# She-Monk

## Sally Thurley

First published by Busybird Publishing 2017

Copyright © 2017 Sally Thurley

ISBN
Print: 978-1-925585-22-3
Ebook: 978-1-925585-23-0

Sally Thurley has asserted her right under the Copyright, Designs and Patents Act 1988 to be identified as the author of this work. The information in this book is based on the author's experiences and opinions. The publisher specifically disclaims responsibility for any adverse consequences, which may result from use of the information contained herein. Permission to use information has been sought by the author. Any breaches will be rectified in further editions of the book.

All rights reserved. No part of this publication may be reproduced, stored in or introduced into a retrieval system, or transmitted in any form, or by any means (electronic, mechanical, photocopying, recording or otherwise) without the prior written permission of the author. Any person who does any unauthorised act in relation to this publication may be liable to criminal prosecution and civil claims for damages. Enquiries should be made through the publisher.

Cover image: Kev Howlett, Busybird Publishing
Cover design: Busybird Publishing
Layout and typesetting: Busybird Publishing
Editor: Tom O'Connell

Busybird Publishing
PO Box 855
Eltham Victoria
Australia 3095
www.busybird.com.au

DISCLAIMER: Every effort has been made to correctly attribute all quotes within. Any misattributions are unintentional.

# TESTIMONIALS

'When in dire need of clarity around a major life decision, Sally managed to help me sift through the murkiness when all other paths pursued had failed. Given that I am not particularly spiritually inclined person but lean towards more practical theory-based solutions, I was astounded at the result of her guided meditation. Sally intuitively knew what to ask and when and ensured she was there for me 100% – I don't recommend people unless I believe in their abilities or trust the services or products they provide. Without hesitation, I would recommend Sally who gives so generously of her time, knowledge, experience and heart space.
**Michelle Kuklinski**

'What I love about Sally is she is so effervescent, authentic, gentle and passionate about what she does. Even though some of the principles may appear or sound complicated, she explains them in a very easy to understand manner which makes the learning process so enjoyable. Sally has opened my eyes to a whole new world of wisdom – wisdom which helped me back into my heart and to understand myself on a much deeper level. Sally is an absolute joy to be around. Her love for life and for others is palpable and I would recommend her to anyone who is looking for the essence of "Simplicity of Grace" to be brought into their world. She is a talent like no other and I'm so grateful our paths have met.'
**Kirsten Barfoot Patti**

'Sally has a magnificent way of making you feel at peace. Every week I look forward to her calming nature and contagious smile.'
**Tarhlia Murray**

'From the bottom of my heart, I'm so grateful to have run across such a warm and loving coach. She really cares and seems to get me. I so love the acceptance and spirituality I'm learning from her. Thanks so much!'

**Rhonda Kendrick**


'After one session, Sally had my mind spinning with ideas. Also, she brought me closer to my core values and helped me define my aims in ways I never thought possible. So not only were her ideas spot-on, but the whole process felt truly authentic to me. It pushed me to the cutting-edge of what I could imagine myself doing at my best.  A real eye-opener. So worthwhile.  Now, when I have issues that challenge me, or could potentially de-rail me from my plan, I feel so certain in the "why" of what I'm doing that I get back on track very quickly.  I highly recommend her process to anyone who is serious about taking the next step in their LIFE.'

**Julia Renaud**


'Lakshmi is an incredible resource. One session with her and I have ideas and inspiration to work on for the next month. She has amazing understanding. She has a gift for seeing what you're trying (and failing) to say and helps you clarify what's really going on. Sometimes I think she sees right through me to my highest intentions and cuts away all the self-doubt, confusion, resistance that clouds my vision. There's something magical about the way I feel inspired to move forward after a session with her. If I'm in an emotional hole, she's so gentle, but at the same time, she cuts through my self-pity to show me how strong I really am and inspires me to get out of the rut. I feel like she's so in tune with me.'

**Julie Deitz**

'With Lakshmi's assistance I was able to unravel blocks and emotional resistance, and envision my ideas anew from a space of positivity and freedom. I was able to re-interpret my reality as a place where freedom and love were already present, and thereby remove the mental distractions and stress which had previously been a daily experience. I have found this technique easy to understand and highly relevant. The Spanda model never fails to calm and empower me, and assist me in regaining control over my experience.'

**Phoebe Matich**

'Working with Sally was amazing. I had never done anything like it before, but I was so glad that I went on the journey. She has such a beautiful, calm manner which instantly relaxed me and stopped me thinking about the outside world. Her healing method, helped me look deep down to the actual problems Id been experiencing and enabled me to clear them. Even now, when I'm feeling things are too much, I use some of the great tools Sally showed me, to help ground myself again. She is amazing in every way.'

**Teressa Fisk**

'Working with Sally was profound. She taught me how to tap into my soul's deepest desire. By the end of it I was clear on who I wanted to be, what I wanted to accomplish and how to achieve it. Sally also gave practical tools I can use again and again to remain on purpose. She is very spiritual and has a down-to-earth and compassionate approach. I would highly recommend her to anyone who wishes to find and manifest their reason for being.'

**Lilette Marie**

'The biggest thing I got out of working with Sally, was the ability to dig way beyond what I thought was needed. It actually turned out to be something completely different and deeper, to the thoughts I had initially. Through her series of exercises, I came to see what I really needed to do, to achieve my goals. More importantly, it gave me the courage to take the leap of faith, right out of my comfort zone & throw myself into the unknown. This in turn seems to have set the wheels in motion to make some really drastic, lifestyle changes and embrace my deepest fear of change, turning it into enthusiasm for the future. I'm feeling motivated for the first time in ages. Everything has come together so beautifully for me.'

**Sumitra Bateman**

*To Magnus and Astrid, my greatest teachers, best friends and the reason for my transcendence and transformation into the best me possible. I love you.*

# CONTENTS

| | |
|---|---:|
| Introduction | i |
| Chapter One – Magic Happens | 1 |
| Chapter Two – Finding Acceptance | 13 |
| Chapter Three – Highest Want | 23 |
| Chapter Four – Your Manifesto | 35 |
| Chapter Five – Soul Calling | 47 |
| Chapter Six – Spirit Tools | 63 |
| Chapter Seven – Beyond Myths | 77 |
| Chapter Eight – Following Grace | 93 |
| Chapter Nine – Inner Creator | 105 |
| Chapter Ten – Mystical Words | 117 |
| Chapter Eleven – Transcend, Transform | 129 |
| Chapter Twelve – Home Temple | 141 |
| Afterword | 161 |
| Thank You | 165 |
| About the Author | 167 |
| Special Offers | 169 |

# INTRODUCTION

This book is for those deeply spiritual beings who've chosen to have a home life and heeded the calling to participate in the world. The idea of a monastery in the Himalayas sounds tantalising, but it's no more so than the passion and fascination of finding and being God while living in the world, as they are with their families, homes and careers.

This book is for those who are spiritual – I'm talking deep, mystical, communion spirituality – with an unashamed love of all things God and the play of consciousness. The original kind of faith: the love of mystical mastery and grace. It's for those who know that there is a place inside of them that everything springs from and that place is universal. This book is for those who have a calling to the world as a spiritual being. It's for those who want to realise themselves and become love; for those who wish to heal, give and receive love; and for those who wish to be the conduit of consciousness. I'm not saying we want to take over the world. This is about the private workings of our inner world, about being perfectly okay with who we are and letting our connection to the divine help others have the same experience.

It's between the divine and us. However that manifests is perfect. There is no right or wrong; there is only what flows through us and our ability to honour and follow it.

This is for you if you find joy and excitement in bringing awareness and light to the world around you. It's for you if you want to be the best you, the spiritual you in your world – the 'I AM'. That is the ultimate success of a She-Monk: to be the I AM, with a partner, kids, career and mission.

You have already had a lot of life experience. As my mother used to say, in this day and age we have earned our badge and blazer once we have gone through and survived life's difficulties, like loss, separation, divorce, illness, etc. Maybe you can sense it has become possible to feel both spiritual desires and fulfil your roles in the world. You want these goals and experiences to empower and inspire. There must be more than this grind, the suffering, chaos and stress that is prevalent in the world today. You've had enough. There must be another way that's more practical and helpful than wandering off into the forest on a spiritual quest or shutting ourselves away in a spiritual centre for years.

"Deeply," you are saying. "Enough. Enough! It is time to give myself permission to be me, the I AM that is trying to express itself in all its glory, through me, as me."

To create world peace we need to start within ourselves. Surely there is an art of living where we become those transforming, divine agents of peace and love? I see the She-Monk as a journey of self-discovery and I'm talking both selves: capital S and little s.

The motivation is the I AM. But first we must learn about who our person is. What is our personhood? Until we learn, recognise and own our given and inherited natures, we cannot fully be us; we cannot be fully aware, self-responsible or heal and integrate ourselves and our world.

This is a new era of consciousness and the state of fear on the planet is at an all-time high. We're all fearful, we're all exhausted, and we're all stressed. Doing our work away in the caves of the Himalayas, or in monasteries and ashrams is no longer the best use of that calling and effort. We need peace on the ground now. Guerrilla peace corps!

The Dalai Lama once said that self-imposed isolation is no longer of use to humanity; the monks need to come out and participate in the world. This resonated strongly with me. So much so that I saw this is what I was trying to manifest as my business calling. I came up with world-monk, She-Monk, domestic-monk and names like that ages ago but business mentors at the time pushed me more into what others were doing. They didn't pick up how special and relevant what I was trying to express was.

I've always been a spiritual being my whole life. I love it and it's the thing I'm best at – communing and hanging out with spirit. I didn't own it earlier because I didn't know it could be a gift. It seemed too natural to be one. It's a wonderful intentionality to want to know the Self and the mysteries of the universe. It's good to ask things like 'Why am I here?' For me it was 'Why am I going through this?' Asking that was my turning point. I was brought up in a non-devotional Anglican family. We worshipped and attended Sunday school because it was expected, because everyone else did it.

I knew I loved God as early as I could remember, but never got the answers I needed. Even at an early age I was frustrated. I knew there was more and I grew sick and tired of the dry lectures and boring interpretations of the scriptures. Instinctively I knew there was something bigger and better. I needed answers and wanted a deeper experience. I was a kid. I believed in magic and always felt a relationship with God, whatever that was.

At eleven I had my awakening, and at sixteen I heard my first wisdom teaching. The mother of a friend of mine did a talk at school. She was a Buddhist, though I had no idea what this was. I asked her what her talk would be about and she said karma and things like how we choose our parents. That was the first time I'd heard anything like this since I was eleven years old and having a huge download about karma. I wanted more.

Eventually, I found my teacher. One day a doctor suggested I learn how to meditate and handed me a pamphlet to a local centre. I joined what turned out to be an ashram and stayed with it for literally twenty years. I questioned, I rebelled, I debated, I participated, I pulled away, I doubted and eventually I surrendered. This path had the tools and everything I needed. For the first time I knew this was something I needed to stick at and not give up on.

This is where my entrepreneurial world-loving nature and spirit had to take a back seat. I had to find how it would work for me, all my passions and the sides to my personality. My frustrations at the centre had to do with some of their outdated attitudes. Householders like me, as opposed to the monks or swamis who lived there, did so much of the heavy lifting and donating, but there was a feeling that we were of secondary importance. Amazingly, some honestly believed that people who were householders couldn't possibly get what those who were living in the grace of the ashram had. People with one foot in the world were susceptible to 'bhoga' or pleasure and enjoyment in the world, which can hook people into delusion and suffering. Yet I saw it was just the same for those pulling themselves away from the world. To me I didn't see that as meritable; I saw it as putting off the inevitable. I had a natural inclination to use the world as my experiment, my playground. I got the best results and deepened my understanding of the teachings by taking what I'd learned and experienced in the ashram and finding how it translated in the world.

I saw as I studied and travelled that this was common in all faiths. The highest and purest was a monk, the lesser was a householder. And it never sat well for me. My BS meter was up. I could see how this may have been the case at a certain point in time, but in this wonderful era of personal freedom, and with the evolving roles of men and women, the opportunity to be graceful, enlightened and living in the world is not only possible, it's available.

I could also see that many of the monks were not necessarily more spiritual nor did they have more attainment; they just had different circumstances and coloured clothes. They didn't all stick to the conditions and rules of taking monkhood either, which stated a life of celibacy and poverty. Many had partners and jobs! It was confusing. I started to question the status quo and saw it was time to re-think the use of the old system. I wondered what is more true and authentic in this age and why anyone would take on of something at that level if they weren't authentically involved? I'd rather be me and own my nature while being committed to absorption in the Self.

I questioned whether the troublesome history of priesthood and the problems of certain gurus arose because it was actually unhealthy to deny the world and not learn how to live in it. Love and abundance are all natural states of God. They are simply energy. Why isn't it possible to learn how to use and deal with them at once? Why must we abolish them completely from our experience?

I see and have experienced that the dedication and commitment we demonstrate when offering ourselves to the service of God is beneficial for our practice. It also builds the energy that can transform us in the world. However, there's no longer any need to recoil from what is fundamentally also our true nature.

During a crucial point in my sadhana, or spiritual practice, my teacher said something that surprised and relieved me. After a trip to India I began having deep experiences. I'd heard a calling to go within, and was naturally drawn to do intense, daily schedules and consistent practice. It was paying off. I'd spend routinely committed time in meditation, prayer and puja (offering) and then head off to work in a café until it was time to pick my kids up from school. I'd continue the practice silently even while working.

I told my teacher I was confused because I was getting intel from the universe and was starting to know who I was: the Self. The only thing stopping me from establishing in the Self were the belief systems I had heard, the spiritual bullshit. The consciousness I was communing with made no distinctions about whether I was male or female, whether I lived in a household or went to an ashram, or whether I was tall, short, fat, skinny, blonde or dark. These superficialities had nothing to do with it. I was the kind of person who liked to do things the right way and here was the universe showing me that nothing meant anything.

One day I asked him sincerely if it was possible then in this faith for a single, working and devotional mother, who worked in a café, did sava (voluntary work or spiritual practice in action), paid her mortgage and dealt with family issues to find the Self, to find the liberation in the midst of all that. He looked at me with total acknowledgement. He smiled happily. He'd been watching and told me about the Rishis of ancient India, that there was a time when householders, men and women were equal. They were liberated while living in the home and contributed greatly to the evolution of spirituality in India.

I had never heard this and went straight home to look it up.

What I got out of that was that nothing is holding us back but us and the garbage we've been told. The rishis came in a time way before monkhood was invented. Yes, monkhood was an invention. So for me the idea of a monk was up for grabs. I think that if we're called to take on that level of commitment and experience then we can; we don't need to change as much as we think.

We become She-Monks. I went down the path of using the name of God as a mantra and connection to a great being. Others prefer mindfulness or to see the world as an illusion. It doesn't matter what you call it because it is the unfolding and the faith that will get you what you need.

My home had become my own temple, my monastery or ashram, a place filled with grace. I had a lot of love in that space; it was a tiny, suburban, average, regular home. Every day at the same time I'd light lights and do mantra and meditate religiously. I didn't have to leave.

I found a way to get myself into the present moment while at home with children running around. It was something the kids loved too, because I made it normal. My routine wasn't loopy or 'religious' and hard-core.

It was cool and different without any strictness or dogma. It was doing it like you'd brush teeth and take the dog for a walk – no big deal. Yes, they rebelled as teenagers but now they miss it and often say how much they love the colour and nectar that came with it.

Then came another turning point. After the above experience the world called, as can happen for some. I really think that for all of us who are deeply spiritual, to function in the world is a whole other ball game! It was okay when I could dance blissfully being a chef in an ashram kitchen. But things really started to go south for me when the universe said, "There's something more for you and it's not staying in here."

During a meditation I was told it's important to find my own way now and become independent. This was God's voice talking to me. It was very stressful. I knew it was time to leave the bosom of the ashram, but there were dogmas and fears about that. One of the weaknesses of many of the old institutions was there was no room for those who were called or empowered from within to do what they needed to do.

Basically I had doubt and fear. I didn't trust the intuition coming through me and I was outsourcing instead to my spiritual community, to my partner, and to my family and friends. But I had pledged to God that I would conquer this. I wanted to heal my life, the external stuff, and overcome the old karmic issues I seemed plagued with. I wanted to work out how to juggle the safety and security of my situation, keep my relationship and have it all in the world.

Big deal, believe me. If you miss the calling it will simply take care of it for you. Trust me! If you wake up one day in a complete mess and total ruin, somewhere along the way you missed a message from the heavens. I own it. I heard the message and overrode it! Please don't do that!

I went through major uncomfortable and unsettling life changes, which went on for about three years. My other fascination was self-development. I have a natural love of it and saw how much it can be missing in spirituality. It sounds really crazy, but it's true. There can be a lot of delusion and spirituality is sometimes used as a weapon, or an excuse to hide. The issue I discovered was that most of the self-development world is success driven. There's not much heart as there's no devotion. I found this exhausting. To me it was full of push instead of pull, even if they were teaching pull. The energy in this world is very harsh, especially when compared to the bells, music, heart, the smell of incense and the singing I was used to. But the answers always come. For me they came hard and loud and I got them.

Welcome to the unfolding of these answers in this book.

## How to use this book!

Here I offer you my gems. These are the personal tactics and inspirations I used, the things that I plucked from my past experiences with different faiths and personal development practices. Here they are all merged.

It's how I became a She-Monk. We can't run away from having to do the painful work of accepting who we are. We must see our flaws and tendencies and be big enough to hold the space of love and healing for ourselves and others to express ourselves.

Just because we can transcend and go to a gorgeous place doesn't mean we stay and hide there. At some stage we have to come back and be in the world. The gift, the skill, is in holding the transcendental experience as we go about our day.

As a She-Monk, this is between you and God, you and your personhood. Or maybe I should say, your personhood and you as God. It's an ongoing dance.

While we're in the body our karmas will play out. Life will never be totally rosy, which I'll elaborate on as we go, but we can find happiness and peace and we can have the love and dedication of a monk. I won't kid you and say that it's an easy path. It isn't because it's one of integration, not separation. We will have to regularly face those things that monks traditionally abstained from so it makes sense it will take tremendous skill and effort to be vigilant and on practice.

It is possible though. Here I ask you to create the environment for divine interaction, to hold your soul's wants, your highest desire and use it to be your intention and relationship with others. I ask that you do the classic practices like forgiveness. Move every experience back to God's perspective and bring that unity back to the world.

Following these will reveal the in-between steps you need to take, the right action. It's different for everyone. You will have your own practice, but I'm asking you to prioritise these general formulas. Eventually our life really does become a state of meditation.

I don't believe there will ever come a time when we don't need a guide, a teacher and a mentor to spiritually help us. Why do people think they can do possibly the most esoteric and obscure thing possible, which really nobody has any idea about, like live spiritually and attain the Self without guidance and grace? So many 'self-realised' teachers I hear doing the rounds today don't seem to get that they may have liberated one area of their being but are far from self-realised. It's clear in how they talk. Hence why it's so important to remain humble and open to learning.

Life is a continuous journey. None of us get off the bus, so to speak. There is always more to learn and to experience and to evolve from. I had a spontaneous awakening as a young kid. This doesn't mean I had all the answers; I still wanted to know more and chose the journey home. An early awakening simply meant that I'd done a lot of the work in a past life. I needed more and was more than happy in this life to immerse myself into what was most comfortable and familiar to me – being in the company of grace.

We'll always need guidance until we become the guide. Although I chose what was right for me, plenty of things still didn't work for me at the ashram. This really drove me crazy, but deep down I knew it could give me everything that I needed on the most important level. And it did, until it was time to move on. In fact, the universe did move me on.

I still seek counsel at times. Hear me: life will give you everything you need. It's rich pickings. There's plenty of fruit out there for a spiritual aspirant. The practice will give you the momentum and build the energy. You resolve to be a good person, which is a choice. Being the best you, with the world mirroring you, will show you where the monk work needs to be done. It's fantastic. I love you just the way you are. I'm not saying you need to become anything other than I AM and let that manifest, because you will. If you have a dream, go for it. If you feel the calling, throw everything you have at it. Live, be in the world, and remember: don't be of it. You are the She-Monk. Your relationship is with the universe and it spills over into the play of your life.

Know when to walk away from something. When you're pushing for change or an outcome, let it go. Live and surrender to God still, however that is for you. Whatever that image or energy that is for you.

I'm delighted to be of service. Be happy and live gracefully.

## Chapter One
# MAGIC HAPPENS

Take a step back. Find out who you are on a soul and physical level. I discovered that the freedom that came with recognition, understanding and being totally okay with me in every aspect was the beginning to great magic in my life.

As a She-Monk you are recognising and surrendering to the call to be the best you possible, to do something wonderful, live the best life, all the while being totally devoted to God, to spirit. You will have the level of commitment of a monk. It's about healing and doing whatever it takes to have spirit flowing through you, as you, with humility and grace.

To let life be the teacher and the home be the ashram. Doesn't get more gorgeous than that.

The magic happens when we remember that we are spirit manifesting due to our awareness in this world. Everything comes from us and dissolves into us. If there are perceived problems they come from not knowing who we are, what we want, what we believe and our unique perspectives and personalities. I saw the need to come to terms with the parts of me that needed integrating. We honestly and sincerely need to learn who we really are – the good, the bad, the beautiful, the ugly – and to find the okayness with it.

We must still take the time that we would take if we were in the monastery. We may no longer be monks in the Himalayas, we're no longer in the ashram, but we are that in the world, we are the I AM. We need to come from spirit, energy and self. Why? Because this is how life will be amazing. Just because we're She-Monks doesn't mean we have to fully merge into playing the traditional roles and models in the world. That, to me, is very appealing. I'm not saying follow the pack here! I'm saying be you!

Sometimes we need to recognise and come to terms with who we really are and our tendencies. We need to recognise when something in ourselves and our lives needs to heal. Often life will throw us into difficult situations until we get this. If we are blaming anything outside of ourselves then we are not doing this properly. In fact, if you're deflecting blame then now is the time to work out your part in the struggle and what you can do to move it to grace.

When we step into who we really are life may get a little bit rougher before it gets better. That's a compassionate little heads-up. There will also be magic, grace, miracles, universal love and support, and a whole new perspective. The good news is that even in difficult situations you will be living in a way you never thought possible.

When we know who we are, things start to come to us from a universal perspective and a bigger picture. We start to get how we can work with pure will, divine will, God's will in a state of surrender. This gives us hope and pure inspiration. That pure creativity, the divine pulse of the universe, and everything else, will reveal itself, step by step, each and every part of the way. We can only do this by being aware and in the moment. The key to divine life is to be present.

To be a She-Monk we will prioritise and master being present. The loss of the sacred in our communities and families has had a huge impact on our culture. We need to bring back the positive and stabilising influence of faith, without necessarily the inhibitions of religion, to help us and our families function and heal.

Once upon a time we had routine in the community. A quiet family day and healthy values give us guidance and the ability to hold onto life's magic and miracles. Life was a miracle and even though it was time to move away from religion some of us have also left the miracle and the magic behind. And this magic can be rediscovered when we identify who we *really* are, who we're being and when we claim the She-Monk and live in the world.

We don't need to follow someone else's script to the letter any more, but we do need to be proactive in bringing back holistic, wholesome living as part of healing and respecting ourselves and the planet.

> 'Knowing others is intelligence; knowing yourself is true wisdom. Mastering others is strength; mastering yourself is true power.'
> **– Lao Tzu**

This is where the magic happens, my darling.

If we are not in service to the divine then we are not in service to anybody, least of all ourselves. We become stressed, anxious and fearful, and we're caught in an overwhelmed and confused state.

There is too great a chance of a life not lived when we aren't led by life's big questions and the call to be love and action. We don't need to fully give up our practice; we don't need to give up that commitment to being as devotional as a monk. To live in the world, we need to always remember who we are and work with the physicality and personality we've been given. I can't tell you the freedom and self-love that has come to me by being okay with how I've manifested and respecting my nature rather than forcing myself to be like others to fit in.

Grace overcomes ignorance. All suffering is ignorance, and ignorance can mean not knowing who we are. Knowing ourselves is fundamental. I'm reminded here of the ancient Greek aphorism 'know thyself'. When we don't, we are living unconsciously. We blame, we are at the whim of others, we become victims and we are dull. We reject who we are … How awful is that? This push is what causes us so much of our grief and so much of our stress. We try to control and manipulate the world, its flow and everybody else around us. Fortunately, as She-Monks we can stop the push and begin to honour what is rising within us. We are more in the flow of life. Life becomes an adventure, an unfolding of grace and magic. In full surrender we are also in control of who we are and how it impacts and inspires others. Seriously, magic really happens.

What is this really about? Magic happens? It's about getting real. That's what this chapter is all about. Getting real is a confession and an admission that things aren't as we pretend they are, or what they could be. Living what is acceptable or to fit in with the wants and needs of others is not coming from spirit, but doing what is called through us as an act of service and love to humanity is. The magic happens when we face who we are squarely, and accept our tendencies, wounds, beliefs and values. We accept our personalities, we accept our karmas – all the things that have happened to us that we usually want to shut down – and we know what we do and don't want.

We must do this before we can become leaders of grace in the home or community, let alone within ourselves. It's a fundamental step. Who am I – both spiritually and as a human being, fulfilling out of what I chose to and created before coming into this life. A role, a purpose, my soul's evolution. We are given our personality to heal. Can you see that? How clever. The crappy stuff is all grist for the mill. As Marianne Williamson says, it's a divine assignment. All we need to learn and overcome is tied up not only in our experiences with others and the world, but in our very natures! Why reject our personhood? There is so much compassion to be gained from accepting and being okay with who we are and we most certainty can integrate and heal the disagreeable stuff.

> 'The journey of consciousness, of mysticism, is to come to know yourself and your own motivations.'
> **– Carolyn Myss**

The first part of any healing is to stop and come to the point where we look at ourselves and say, "What is happening here? How am I responsible? What am I doing? What is really true?" Until we make that small but huge leap in perspective and vision we end up running in a loop. Even though we've done a lot of spiritual work, even though we're dedicated as spiritual beings, it doesn't always translate in the world. We can get just as hooked in, make just as many mistakes and have a lot of inauthenticity and integrity issues.

I remember when I was a single mum and had two small kids at primary school. I was going through huge changes and having spiritual experiences, but I was still a mother and things really weren't perfect. It was a real surprise. Life didn't magically get better! In fact, things got a little harder. But here I am. I've been in and out of spiritual teachings and communities for all these years and done so much work. I've also done a lot of personal development work. There was a time when I would look at my life and realise that I had this despair. My relationships didn't work and I was still grieving the loss of my mother and the impact this had on my family. On the surface I've always been a happy-go-lucky capable kind of person so I don't think people realised that things weren't all that great with me and that perhaps something was missing.

I desperately wanted at that time to have the life that I felt I could have but I didn't know what that was because some of my personal tendencies were so enormous and were getting in the way. What I really knew was that I wanted to have a healthy, worldly life. I wanted that right partner and I wanted to get out of being a broke, single mum in the back suburbs. I knew that having a deep spirituality didn't mean I had to be broke. I didn't need that old world way of looking at spirituality. I was looking outside myself at that stage for a miracle. I was looking to my guru, to my community, for a partner to fix everything; I was looking for the right job, the right money. At some point I laid down in my room and said to myself, "I need a miracle. What has happened to the magic?" The answer I got was that it was time to grab life by the horns. Complaining about pain and the suffering was a waste of time. It was time to start changing some patterns, but for that to happen I first had to see and own them.

This was my first step: claiming and owning who I really was so I could be the best me. That was my decision. I was going to get real about what I was bringing to the table. I made a pledge to God to be the best me. This painful journey took time, as all good journeys do. It didn't happen overnight; it took many years actually. There was always more to learn. Situations were set up for me to experience so that I could work in each and every moment and bring in a new awareness. I started facing my personhood issues with the grace of also knowing myself on a soul level. My big issues at that time were dealing with a lot of childhood hurt and gaining emotional resilience.

I've noticed many 'deeply' spiritual people aren't really authentic about who they are. It used to worry me when I'd see teachers, yogis, swamis and monks getting angry or upset and even being abusive and taking it out on those around them. This wouldn't worry me as much if they had a sense of humour about who they were and could admit their mistakes, but I've heard them say they have transcended this kind of behaviour!

Some of us have a lot to overcome, especially from traumas. Not knowing how to deal with big emotions and dealing by hiding or denial makes things so much worse. I realised that being free didn't just depend on spending time with my highest self; it started with who was I being and figuring out how I could still love myself.

In relationships, I realised that I was playing out my pain body. In other words I was letting unconscious wounds speak for me. My pain body was huge. I was playing out the hurt from my childhood and wanting a man to take over and look after me. I wanted security. I'd hold out, holding in the disappointments and emotions and bursting forth with frustration every now and then. I'd expect others to understand me and wanted unconsciously to be taken care of.

My spiritual world was fantastic. I was having amazing experiences; I was already a great meditator and had a one-on-one relationship with God. This relationship was completely fulfilling but it hadn't magically made me into something obviously glorious nor had it necessarily translated on every level into my worldly life. There is a lot of delusion here in thinking that awakening or liberation will make us magical mystical all-powerful fairies. More about that in my spiritual BS chapter.

How did I start to accept and understand who I was on a human level? I looked to every typology there was to get the answers. They are there for a reason and they are wonderful. I'm not saying they hold all the answers – some of them are very broad – but we can go in and extract the nectar and what resonates. Not all will fit for you and it will depend on your source of information so get the best you can. There are plenty of great systems and typologies out there. First of all, I went and got my natal astrology chart done. I learnt that there were things about me that were meant to happen. I was meant to have this personality. What I saw as a curse was actually a gift. It was so uplifting! Hooray! I was squeezing myself into an expectation from my family and community and it wasn't their fault; it's just how they operated. But I was different and, in hearing this, I felt tremendous relief and healing. Magic literally followed.

It helped me own things and helped me find peace with what I thought were terrible traits. They weren't that bad after all. I also found other traits that I didn't know I had and started to see how they are not set in stone, that I can, in fact, transform and change them. The best I came across was the Enneagram, which was an ancient mystical system of handing down how to work with the different personalities of devotees from teacher to teacher. A good teacher or guru would know the personality type of their devotee and would package the teaching in a way that would be best received by them. These three types were mental, physical and emotional. From that came the Enneagram, which helped me understand my personality in a very liberating way.

How can we master ourselves and contribute soundly in the world until we master our relationship with our minds, our physicality and our emotions? There is no one-size-fits-all. Every approach is unique and we all need to investigate as much as we can and work it out for ourselves. Other wonderful and helpful typology systems are: Numerology, Myers Briggs, VAK learning styles, archetypes.

Let's not forget therapy. There's nothing wrong with needing therapy. It's not easy to understand our 'human' at times. It can be refreshing and helpful to have a safe space to empty our cup and to get a fresh perspective or, even better, some good feedback. When we are doing spiritual work, we often transcend the body and forget to really look at it. We transcend what is happening in our world instead of really investigating what we are bringing to our experience, both good and bad. I wished a lot more people around me had access to therapy, particularly in spiritual communities. Therapy helped me understand who I was and showed me that the things I needed to overcome were also gifts.

Once I knew all this, the real juice was in acceptance. I had to own it, be okay with who I was. Bring it back into myself. No more painting on spots when I really had stripes, no more letting others criticise me for not being practical or methodical when I was artistic and highly creative. Interestingly, the more I owned and accepted who I was, the more my passion and capabilities began to emerge. If I slipped back into an old way of being or a negative trait, I'd be okay. Instead of shaming or beating myself up, I'd talk to it, hug it and peace would return. It took ages to work this out and it did mean people who were not healthy for me left or I had to gracefully move away from them. That happens when we become responsible for who we are and take ownership.

And as soon as I said, "Enough! I'm willing to look at myself and be okay with who I am. It's time for a miracle. It's time for some money. It's time for a new job," things changed. Everything got cleaned up, one by one and each situation gave me the opportunity to become more emotionally resilient. That was what I most needed to work on. The benefit of knowing things like who we are, and getting insights and understandings, then helps us to see others. We become so much more compassionate. We can also empower them to go through the same process. It's so healing.

When I got my mother's birth chart done, only this year, I felt the most astonishing compassion for her. It was almost too much because for the first time I understood her in a way that I never could before. My mother and I had a tumultuous relationship. It was a psychotic relationship, with a lot of mental and physical disharmony. When I finally got her birth time I discovered she was a very tortured soul who was in a lot of pain. So much love and acceptance started to flow through me. I wish I had known this while she was alive because I would have tried to find a way to talk to her and help her.

It's been so helpful knowing who my kids are, what their personalities and some of their karmas are, and what makes them tick. I now know that they behave in certain ways because that is their particular way to express something. This helps me bring in a lot of compassion and tolerance. I can also gently point them to a more empowering place, which was really handy during their teen years.

In my spiritual community I saw some meditators who were extremely functional and happy in that environment. Yet they couldn't work, let alone function, in the outside world. Some of them were hiding out there and coming up with excuses like, "Oh well, you can't be spiritual in the world. You'll lose it. You'll get consumed by the world." This is an 'old-world' spiritual viewpoint that can have some truth to it, but I think in their case it was a cover because they didn't want to go out and participate. I saw that hiding behind the robes and the institution was not an authentic way of living. Unless, of course, you could really own it and be okay with it and it was really what the universe was asking of you. Can you see that distinction?

I met people who were considered great teachers or 'acharyas'. They had been successful in the world, but they never did the emotional work, the work of being human. They weren't compassionate and understanding and didn't listen to their partners and children, let alone fess up to what they wanted to do and be. It was a trip and, in some cases, I saw how spirituality could become a tool or a weapon. When I was doing a personal development course I saw that I had this unique skill of brushing people off and brushing off what they were doing. I'd say, "Well, in the spiritual world we don't do this." Fortunately, it was pointed out to me that I was using my spirituality as a leveraging tool in an unholy way.

The goal of the She-Monk isn't to be a powerhouse of human achievement, though she does need to know and honour who she is. That's a choice and we need to move in that direction and make the effort. The She-Monk is happy to love, to be love, to be the aspects of the divine feminine and to be happy. She is the I AM. Happiness doesn't come from success. In fact, there is a simpler level before even talking about success. Happiness, relief, peace, self-love comes from knowing and accepting who you are and finding ways to have others to do the same. Therein lies the magic. I guess you could say it's when we look at ourselves and say, "I am willing to take my life into my hands and get real about who I am and what I am contributing to my word. I'm going to give up using it to make myself feel worse or a lost cause. I am going to be okay with it and start to heal."

We must look at who we really are, as both a soul and a person, then accept what we discover with love. This is step one to not only healing and integration, but to being a She-Monk.

## What if I'm ostracised?

I totally hear you. You mean what if I'm rejected by the tribes I belong to because I'm moving beyond them? This can happen. Sometimes living empowered lives and being honest, transparent and fully responsible for who we are can be intimidating for others, as they might not be ready to behave in the same way. If relationships end as a result, let them go with love, compassion and as little roadkill as possible. It's crazy but acceptance isn't something we are taught. So when we are okay with how things are this can really push others into a cycle of anxiety, stress, anger and depression, it shows what they need to discover and work on.

Sometimes, also we are no longer a match with others, even family. Generally, though, I'd say that by being the best you possible, by getting real with who you are and finding love and acceptance, you will save relationships and create a beautiful living environment for those you love. If you are honest then at least you can clean up as you go along and be left with little residue. Don't get hung up about being ostracised. See that is fear and move to trusting God at the capacity that a She-Monk needs to trust. Remember, spirit first. In faith, everything will unfold as it should. If some branches are meant to be trimmed or maybe even spontaneously drop from our tree it is okay. More light can get through ;-)

## I was told growing up that we make our own bed so must lie in it.

This basically means 'I am this way and therefore need to sit in the consequences of that'. That's a shocker, isn't it? In some ways, yes, we do need to be responsible for the consequences in our lives, such as poor behaviour and bad decision-making. However, this doesn't mean that we are forever cursed with those decisions. We are always free to create the life and situation we want and we are always able to change a situation. If we can't accept or change it, then it's time to leave it. Get to know what it is in you that creates certain situations and accept it, but don't think this means you must sit in a mud puddle of punishment. This is about freedom of being. It's about healing our person, evolving our soul, clearing karmas and bringing in awareness and owning who we are. We are never stuck or hopeless; there is always hope.

Some people are scared of change and don't think that they're strong enough to admit who they really are or what they really want. Yet here is where the magic happens. A She-Monk needs to be humble. She needs to be able to put her ego aside to be a servant of God in the world. This can be very scary as change is daunting at first. It's a form of uncertainty. When we live with uncertainty we are, in fact, living creatively and in the Tao of the universe.

Remember who you are. Have faith. Whatever happened has presented itself to you for you to grow and learn. You are more than able to handle it. It's part of your evolution and divine assignment. So get help. Please never think that you are beyond help. Liberated people *need* help. Sometimes people need help with their mindset and emotions, and this is also true of spiritual people.

You need to take everything that happens to you as a learning opportunity. That way you will become the best you possible. You will never look back. Life will be a whole lot better and the healing that will take place is beyond your wildest imagination, so stick to that as inspiration. The desire to be the best you possible comes in that moment when you realise, 'Oh my god, life isn't what I wanted it to be.' Being spiritual didn't cure or help me. Personal development work didn't totally help me. There is something in me that has to come from the inside out. It needs to be a decision. To be a She-Monk is a choice, but we can't hide behind it; we can't use it as an excuse to be authoritative. We're simply taking that dedication, that humility, to the world.

The first step is to pray to God and announce that you want to be the best you possible. Meditate on it and see what comes up. What areas are up for review? What can you learn about yourself? What do you indulge in that causes disharmony and what can you own? What do you need to work on and bring the light of the Self to? What needs healing? We all need to work on aspects of ourselves till the day we die. There is never a moment in our physical body when there isn't something to learn.

List your spiritual practices and your toolkit. What do you do every day? How dedicated are you? Do you compromise? Why? Do you have a mentor? If not, find one. We all need a mentor, particularly for our spiritual journey. When we leave the so-called temples, ashrams and monasteries, we still need someone we can commune with and receive advice from. We need people who have walked the path already. I highly recommend finding a community of like-minded people.

Dive into finding more about yourself. Keep a journal. Start watching the patterns. What are your core beliefs and values and what impact do they have on you and others? Work out your personhood. If you know your birth time have a look at astrology. What is your Enneagram number? Hey, what is your numerology? It all helps. Remember, make sure you find the best sources, as there's a lot of crap out there.

A She-Monk knows who she is and she admits it. You want to turn your life around and know who you are? You already know who you are. You are God. We've done that part. This is where we take that I Am to the world and see how our personalities perform. First we must see where our stumbling blocks and weaknesses are.

Don't panic and make more meaning if you discover that you don't have such a nice personality. Deep down inside there is the right manifestation of it. Prayer, meditation and being loving will bring that out so have a look and don't hold it back. Let it out and get help. Be an example to others.

## Chapter Two

# FINDING ACCEPTANCE

One of the main reasons we don't do the work to find out who we really are is we are hesitant to accept what we have within us or what has happened to us. But this is God-given and a part of our divine setup. Maybe we want to be someone else or we are ashamed or embarrassed. Whatever it is, we push who we are away rather than embracing it and seeing what mystical alchemy takes place when we do so. We want to reject; we'd rather be ignorant to it.

I discovered that being profoundly okay with the present moment, as it is, was a path to healing and mastery. Sounds perfectly obvious, but I needed the word 'okay' to really get it. Acceptance was something really new for me. It wasn't part of the tradition I'd come from so I'd never had much to do with it. I could transcend beautifully but had no idea how to integrate my personality and experience at such a basic and compassionate level. When I adopted this practice as an experiment and last resort, I saw that the path of freedom and least resistance was to accept and be okay with my disability at that time, to allow myself to be depressed and isolated and have different mystical experiences. I suddenly understood this whole presence and healing thing on a totally new level.

When we can be completely okay with everything about us and

everything that is happening to us we are, in fact, living in the eternal moment. We are not fighting with the universe and exhausting ourselves in the process.

Self-acceptance is an act of self-love, the greatest act of self-love. When we sit down and say, "Okay, I'm not going to change this. I'm not going to fight this. I'm not going to judge myself. I'm not going to beat myself up for having this tendency or personality or illness." This creates the space for healing and divine intervention. It actually acts as a circuit breaker for the story or the drama.

It brings in what I call a seluvial space. Seluvial is a word I created to describe when I put a ring of consciousness around me. It's like a buffer that I hold as sacred and it protects me when I'm dealing with things like time and people. I become more present and have healthier boundaries. This means that I slow down more into that eternal moment and I gain the ability to make better choices and better decisions; I think before I act. I imagine this seluvial space as a doughnut of grace, or one of those swimming rings we have as children. If I let the world into that space by not being vigilant and present, then I usually suffer. I was one of those kids with no boundaries; I wasn't allowed to have them as a child so I let everything in. Everything. Now I have something I can feel and visualise. If that space was threatened, then I knew to say no. Simple as that. Total game-changer.

Instead of being triggered we can now accept our situation, allowing us to soften our reactions and enter a zone where we can say, "Okay, this is what's happening. How do I wish to react? What do I need to do?"

We get better at it and it changes with time. It actually plays with time, bringing compassion, awareness and truth. When we accept who we are and what we are going through, we reconnect with things like our breath, our energy, our thoughts and our bodies. We start to pay attention to what we do and how we do it. This is the path to integrating and becoming whole, hence healing. Once we know what we do, why we do it and what our triggers are we can move to acceptance and gratitude. We can really, really, really see it all as one. We are the entire play of the universe expressed a certain way.

> 'We are here as She-Monks because we want the peace and equanimity of a monk and the joy and wonder of a child in the midst of our worldly life.'
>
> **– Me**

We keep ourselves in low-grade suffering and pain because we usually disown part of ourselves. Here is a major cause of anxiety, if not *the* cause. We are pushing away the memories, experiences, emotions, thoughts and actions that we don't want to experience or own. Hence we suffer. We feel discontentment, become stressed and depressed, and develop anxiety.

Stress is the modern epidemic. One in three Australians suffer from anxiety! Mostly women. We don't live fully. We shuffle our experience and our personhood around and we hide from who we are. A She-Monk won't tolerate that. In fact, with the daily routines and commitments to God and Self, we find we no longer can. It is part of taking our practice and experience to another level.

By not accepting ourselves and our world, we tell our brains and bodies that we are flawed, that we aren't good enough, that we're frauds and that everything is wrong. When we don't accept we are telling a lie. Our brains take on our beliefs and help us to create more of the same experience. Our cells in our bodies hear the inner talk, feel the angst and respond with inflammation and disease. Seriously, can you picture this? Can you feel it? What is your body saying to you? Do you ever sit and listen to it? Acceptance is healing.

When we see things as good or bad through a filter, we are in the judgement mind, whose job is to categorise, decompartmentalise and convince us we are separate. This is also known as the ego. We're broken away from the whole. We wear masks and uniforms to fit in and again we aren't living an authentic life. I don't know too many people who live at that level of authenticity but I do know that in this new millennium and era of consciousness it's becoming a requirement. Authenticity and transparency are popular new buzzwords. Thank God! To be able to laugh at yourself, to know that you've been a bit of an idiot in a particular situation, to be able to say to someone in a really empowered way, "I really get what I did just then and how it created this situation and I'm truly sorry. That wasn't the outcome I intended. I have this tendency sometimes to do X."

Happiness, fulfilling relationships and wellbeing depend on us taking the time to know ourselves and to be okay with ourselves. Otherwise they become elusive. Being okay means being okay in the present moment. That is a state of acceptance, a state of awareness. When we accept our life the way it is and don't try to be someone else then gorgeous things will flow through us, creating change that is beyond our wildest dreams and desires.

And that's because we've stepped into grace.

The beautiful part of acceptance is that it lovingly regroups and welcomes parts of our being that have been dislocated, cut off and made separate. We prevent energy blockages, which is how sickness begins, and we stop being wrong. Who cares if we're wrong? What are we usually fighting for? Acceptance transforms the wrong and brings in compassion. It makes us remarkably human on the most beautiful level.

The seluvial space brings in the spaciousness required to solve problems and prevents us from getting bogged down in shoulds and shouldn'ts. Without it we often fall into blame or throw our hurt onto other people – anything to avoid being seen as responsible and look better than who we really are. We do crazy things. We often 'up' our negative tendencies like anger, manipulation and control just to feel powerful and right. We need to commit to sitting in the present moment in a practice of witnessing consciousness, our higher self and seeing everything for what it is. When we can do this for ourselves, we are powerfully positioned to do this for others.

This is the greatest gift we can give one another: to be able to hold space for them so that they feel our acceptance no matter what. This enables them to have that same experience for themselves. I can't think of a greater act of love. Listen and create space and you'll no longer view the person as wrong, no matter what they have done.

In acceptance we gain clarity and inspiration starts to enter. Most importantly, acceptance means we're in communion with our higher self and our nervous system responds. We move to more parasympathetic living rather than stress. Amazingly, those problems, those issues that have plagued us, become small, become our friends; we laugh with them and then they help us with the answer, the solution. It's incredible.

My biggest experience with learning acceptance was quite traumatic. I fell very ill and the cause of it was a mystery at the time. I was dedicated to my teacher, sadhana and spiritual community, had a health coach business, had a spiritual nutrition and cooking business where I was invited along to multi-faith functions as a nutritional and spiritual chef, and was as a speaker and presenter in the mind-body-spirit arena. I was what you would call healthy. I was teaching about health and wellbeing and then literally overnight I was disabled. I couldn't walk. One day I woke up and my legs wouldn't move. I'd come down with the most terrible arthritis and one thing after another started to happen. When I thought I was going to get better, I suddenly got worse. My body was breaking down. I was getting autoimmune disorders and I had terrible insomnia. My whole system just caved in. I was no longer able to live life as I had. I couldn't do what I enjoyed or go and see people. I now had to say, "I can't come. I can't walk. I'm in too much pain."

People would look at me and say, "But you're a health coach," "But you meditate," or "Spiritual people don't get sick." God, I hated that one. I was mortified that people saw me as a fraud and started to take that on myself because I couldn't work out why this was happening. All that plant-based living, exercise and loving what I did and yet there I was, in the eyes of other people, wrong. I was so down on myself for it. I was disgusted and would beat myself up. After about a month of being literally bed-bound I realised this was unsustainable. There had to be a truth out there, something higher than what myself and others were seeing. I even said to myself, "Well, what if this is as good as it gets?" That, surprisingly, was my first step towards okayness and it brought tremendous relief. I remember eventually calling my teacher and saying, "Please tell me what all this is about."

He said, casually, to look up the great saints, to see what they said and did because they weren't all well. They had disease. They had things happen to them that were horrendous. Brilliant. He was right. All the answers I needed were there and I learnt about Parabda Karma. I completely got it and the fight, the rejecting, stopped. As soon as I took it on board and accepted it, I saw a level of karma that I had only known on a superficial level. We have a divine assignment, something that is meant to happen to us that we created before we take birth. We create situations, throw them out there, that are going to happen because we need them to for the sake of our evolution.

It deepens our being and grounds us profoundly. I realised that's what I was going through and the fruits were extraordinary. It was mystical, beyond the realms of healing. Doctors couldn't work it out. The healers – one or two really good ones – told me this was a spiritual healing crisis. I realised that what I was going through was actually perfect. It was a gift and I began to accept it. I may not walk properly again. I may end up having two knee replacements. The bone-on-bone arthritis was severe but I was too young. I thought, 'Okay, if I spend the next twenty years of my life in a wheelchair, it's going to be okay'. The freedom that came with this completely changed my journey. I ended up becoming open to the divine intel that was coming through me. A better version of me was literally being created from each and every cell up, even my DNA. It certainly was an angelic setup. It was beyond the rational mind so I decided not to get it involved.

I learnt from this experience. Now whenever I help clients accept their situation and feel the sensation in their bodies, they experience huge relief and an emotional release. I had a client not long ago who had been on the mill of healers and therapists. He was very, very uptight. I sat him down and said, "Let's just be okay. What if there's not a problem here? Let's just get terribly present and I want you to witness what you are doing to yourself and the extra stress you are causing yourself." He literally sobbed for the first time in many years. He came with depression and he left without it – all because he stopped fighting and pushing. He sat with it all without judgement and he began to laugh.

It was as though I could feel the gunk jettisoning out of him and he became raw in his heart, which is my favourite place to see anyone. When we go through something significant like that we begin to see the things we've been covering up more clearly. This is very, very humbling. I'd say most of us – ninety percent of us – don't know what it is to live in our heart and be fully okay with ourselves and everybody else. Can you say that you do?

Self-acceptance showed me the awful holes in my body, which I had created by shooting myself with harsh thoughts, such awful thoughts. I was so violent towards myself for getting sick and so easily toppled by other people's nasty comments. They were stuck in spiritual bullshit, spiritual myths, honestly believed that nothing in life would go wrong if you're spiritual and eat well. If it does, you're full of shit – according to them.

I moved from my experience beyond the body consciousness into the mystical healing realm. When I saw how awful I was being to myself, I realised it was time to become okay. I had experienced little self-love my whole life and had become arrogant because I was preoccupied with superficial things like nutrition, exercise and meditation. In the past these had cured pretty much everything for me. Sure, they might be good, but they aren't the whole story. So I began to nurture myself and love me for who I was. To my surprise, the most positive impact this had was on my children.

Our relationships completely transformed. The more I accepted myself, the more they accepted themselves and they started to love themselves more. It was the most fantastic gift. Self-acceptance, as I said, is self-love. From there we need to act on that. What are your versions of self-love? I had never allowed myself to do self-loving activities, like getting a massage or accepting compliments. I discovered my desire for independence. I learnt timeout; before I was always all things to everybody. I stopped the push, learnt to say no, became discerning about the company I kept and moved away from controlling and inauthentic people.

## What if okayness justifies awful behaviour in others?

This is not about justifying. This is about being. This is about getting detached from the drama and the robotic action taking hold of yourself and others and stopping the push to find the real solution. Sadly, delusion is part of being human. In yoga they call it Maya. We all have it to different degrees and it can be a form of hiding from a truth that is too awful in our minds to look at. It is pure concealment of grace.

We all need to become okay with the present moment because we need to be one hundred percent in it to really live. This will reveal the truth in any delusion for someone who's sincere. Rejecting it keeps us from the here and now, whether we consciously realise it or not. Moving to acceptance is a compassionate idea and it is better to have an accepting attitude than to expect others to behave a certain way. Recognising that we have done something that is not in the best interests of ourselves and others is the first step towards finding forgiveness, apologising and creating a new space for awareness and perspective to find a better way of being.

Be fantastically okay with everything life throws at you.

People have an option to follow your example. Always lead by example and focus on yourself not them. By going inward and finding that seluvial space of grace around you, you can ask yourself intelligent questions and inquire into the truth of the matter. By doing this you may find the way to help others.

### I fear that if I accept this it will continue.

It may, but your relationship to it will be different and you will know what to do. Once we have stopped the fight, the push, the fear, grace can enter and perform miracles. In the space of acceptance, the creative power to choose is present and the right solution will present itself. Be really honest with yourself. Once you've looked at the role in your situation and owned who you've been, accept it. Ask your higher Self what is the next best step. Be open and courageous. You may have inadvertently saved the situation and all involved. You may have freed yourself and others from it being continued.

### I don't ever want to be okay with what's happened to me.

Some people don't know how to be okay. They don't even want to entertain the idea of accepting the trauma they've experienced. That's our survival nature or ego trying to look after you in its limited way. It may take time, but you need to have the intention to heal, to not be a victim forever. I'm not being harsh here. I have been there, justifying what has been something traumatic and humiliating, holding onto a righteous story and wanting others to apologise and compensate. It's a bleak way to live and will cause misery and disease. Jump off that ride!

At some stage, the urge for peace will come through you if you stick to your She-Monk commitment. Don't beat yourself up for being at this place. We all have layers of things that need healing and they come up when we least expect it – sometimes just when we think everything is okay.

My advice is to get help. Find a spiritual mentor who will be there for you every step of the way. A spiritual healer can hold the space for acceptance and forgiveness. Surrendering, which acceptance is a form of, is the most liberating act that will free you from the prison of our justifying, survival mind. You know it's possible. There are many stories of those who have healed, accepted and moved forward. Hold at least the possibility as a birth right.

> 'We are always completely free to move to love, to grace, to change our energy and perspective, to evolve. It's simply a choice.'
> **– Osho**

If we can accept all moments with okayness and appreciation, a deep gratitude will seep in. This is how nothing ever really goes wrong. Do you see?

## Three Actions:

All the goodness of the divine grace is found in the present moment, in that eternal moment where anything is possible. Spend time with yourself as you are and simply observe every part of you. Your body, your thoughts, your emotions. Meditate and witness without judgement or control.

Go to my website: www.sallythurley.com/meditations

I like to visualise welcoming the experience, all the emotions and crappy comments I may be thinking, as if I've invited it for afternoon tea. Try that on. Welcome them as guests because if they are in your awareness they simply want your attention and if you can show love then they will no longer have a grip on you. They will be happy and all will return to peace. Know you are given all you need to be able to hold onto your experience. You have what it takes to heal, transcend and transform. Be a stand for peace. Whatever it takes. It takes great practice and usually requires help, which is why it's important to find a spiritual mentor who has been there before.

## Chapter Three
# HIGHEST WANT

Identifying our highest wants takes us to what is truth for us on a soul level. It explains why nothing else will work when trying to be a She-Monk because, unless we are working with our highest want, the rest of our life is not in harmony with what our hearts want. This is the beginning of what became my life's calling and was one of my biggest light-bulb moments.

In discovering this there was a new level of honesty between my heart, my soul and the universe. I got clarity on why I was doing what I was doing, what the real reason behind my behaviours was and what I craved. I got to experience working with pure will in a whole new way. It was a simple switch from the kind of want that seemed obvious, like *I want a car, I want more money,* all that kind of stuff, to what God wanted for me, which was my highest Self.

Once I had worked out what I wanted I could follow the steppingstones back home to the divine in any situation. When you find out what your heart really, really desires and your soul's calling you can have a good shot at breaking the cycle of suffering. It's simple to step out of the mundane circle into joy.

There are many teachings about wants out there. The yogis and Buddhists have been banging on about wants for centuries but sometimes you may hear a teaching over and over again but it's kind of noise until you get it for yourself. That was my relationship with wants. I had to have my own insights to turn it into a transformation tool.

This is where, in a particular moment, you'll say, "Hang on. Is this what I'm really after? Am I doing that? Am I being that? Am I allowing grace to come?" This is such a release for everyone around us and our nervous systems.

When we know and share what we really want from a heart-centred place others will have a better idea of what we're trying to do and the intention behind it. This way they can be on the same page and offer their support and compassion. They may also realise what they really want! We become so much easier to live with.

In the Eastern traditions, which are the wisdom traditions I was brought up in, it is said that suffering is caused by ignorance. Ignorance is part of the play of being human and it amounts to not knowing who we really are, having a closed mind, or not seeing the oneness or highest perspective in a situation. It is when we act unconsciously, when we act outside of the present and without awareness. It's where we don't know what we want.

When coming from ignorance, we usually react from the five senses. We are not aware of our thoughts, emotions, tendencies, personalities, actions and beliefs. Most importantly, we don't know what we really want in our hearts or our calling, contribution to the world we are drawn to. We feel that our true happiness is at stake. The worst part about not knowing what we want from our soul level is we become like the blind leading the blind.

We take on a sheep mentality, sticking within the rules and doing what is seen to be done. We don't really know what makes us happy or what lights us up, nor do we know why we do the things we do. Worse still we do things we really dislike or do things that are purposefully destructive. We tend to be at the whim of others, to beliefs and conditioning and, at the end of the day, that's how we become resentful and full of blame.

> 'When we don't know what we want we can miss our life calling.
> Everything we're doing is to go Home.'
> **– Me**

Everything we want in any moment is to go back home to God, to be God. Don't get hung up on my use of the G word here. I'm really cool with the word God and it brings me joy. You may use what works for you. Try universe if you find that more comfortable.

We want communion with God every day and in every moment and get disconnected from our spirit and heart when we do not own what it is we want. This want is never a superficial thing; it's always something that comes from our soul, that *is* our soul.

When we don't know what we want we can become caught up in expectations. Knowing what we want makes us responsible for it. We see that it is purely up to us to get it. I dig that. I like the freedom that comes with personal responsibility.

Do you know people who are prone to a sense of entitlement? They are driven by a contracted ego and a sense of lower want. "I want this and I'm entitled to have it!" This causes so much pain and is not the truth. We are not entitled to anything. Ever. Not anything on a gross level, anyway. I do think we are all special, though. That's why I find people fascinating. I love them. I love finding what makes them unique and wonderful, even their less than desirable tendencies. I think it's great to be special as in be love. Be you. You're gorgeous, seriously. Many people don't know what to do when I say that to them. Like the woman at the counter who made me a tea. Her gorgeousness was oozing out and I had to tell her. We're all special, but please don't get to thinking you're better or more entitled than anyone else. That's getting off track.

Victimhood is another example. Playing the victim sets us up for disaster because we're not coming from what we most want. We're instead playing into our traumas and wounds, saying, "Woe is me". Victimhood is awful for relationships and is highly dysfunctional. When we know what we want we are being responsible for the happiness, joy and vitality of our life and our relationship with the world around us. We 'outsource' ourselves by handing over our personal remote control to others. We expect them to know what we want and we expect them to do things for us. But acting as though people should be fulfilling our needs puts us in a really disempowered and ugly place. Ever been there? We sometimes do this to another, or even to a group. Heck, we could even be resentful and full of blame for an entire community.

No one should have our remote control. Please don't put that level of pressure on someone else. Even if they think they want it. They don't. It's fundamental that we work this out for ourselves and pursue our own divinely guided path.

As She-Monks, it's part of our work to know what we want.

All we want to do is go home, and we can do that easily when we simply 'purify' our wants. We can bring that want while we're in communion and hold it in place for the rest of our day. Every single one of us – our children, our spouses, our bosses, the postman, the person who's depressed, the person who's happy – thinks they do certain things for pleasure and to avoid pain. But on a higher level we do them to go home. Our souls need to evolve. Our wants hold the key so we return to oneness.

Here's something fabulous: we don't realise it but we can have what we want. And here's the twist: you can expect it! Your soul's want, that is. It's the only thing you can expect, because you're meant to have it; it's an attribute of who you already are! Sit with that for a minute. Take it in. It's awesome. What we want is simply what we already are but have forgotten! When we go after things we mistakenly think we want we end up outside of ourselves. You can never expect anything that isn't in alignment with who you really are.

How did I come to this? I got the greatest clarity when I was trying to solve one of my own life riddles. I was in a relationship with a man I really loved and yet the relationship really sucked. It wasn't working. I could see it was another one about to hit the wall, about to become something in my rear-vision mirror. This wasn't what I wanted. I desperately wanted that relationship to work but couldn't understand what it was in me that was stopping me from getting what I thought I wanted.

One evening when I was sitting in Satsang, a programme with my spiritual community, I heard my teacher talking about how the Buddhists believe ignorance is the root cause of all suffering. He turned and said, "Ignorance is when we don't know what we want or when we reject what we have."

What I heard was that when we don't get what we want, we have a tantrum. Every part of suffering is a form of tantrum. I hear that and laugh. It actually brings me joy and lights me up, even if something bad has happened. I tell myself my reaction is a tantrum because I didn't want it to happen and usually end up laughing. Consider that as soon as we react, we close our heart; as soon as we move into despair and desperation, we move into depression, into anger, into blame, then into victimhood; we have, in effect, thrown a gigantic tantrum, whether justified or not. This blew my brains, so I took this away and contemplated for some time. I sat and contemplated and I said, "Okay, what are my expectations here?" I expect to be loved, I expect to be nurtured, I expect for him to read my mind, and I expect for him to stop any controlling and domineering behaviours.

Stick with me here. It gets even better. It was one of those classic light-bulb moments. An epiphany. I saw that if I boil down what I thought I wanted to a feeling I was chasing, as an attribute of the divine, then that is the truth. I saw that we have different types of wants and they all lead back to home in a particular order. There's the first one, which is what I call a complaint or a 'B want'. That's the realm that most of us live in. I want him to behave, I want my child to stop talking to me like that, I want my partner to be home on time, I want more money, I want a better job, etc. And yet when I cut it down, what is the real thing? It's my soul saying, "Remember a time when I was peace and harmony and love, and all of that never mattered? Remember I was universal consciousness and now I'm somehow limited. But in a crazy way I'm still universal consciousness, which means I am peace, I am harmony. I am love, I am wisdom; I am joy, happiness, wellbeing and all those delicious things." *How cool is that?* Not only is the true meaning behind our complaining but we can actually have it because it's who we really are; it's the truth. That's what we need to aim for. We need to go for it like we've never gone for anything else in our lives. I took that on. I remembered a time I went for a particular divine experience like I already had it because it was in me and I eventually got that experience and everything fitted now into place. I had to bring that certainty and even expectation to what I wanted because if it's about my soul then it's mine already.

Does this make sense to you? Can you see how you can do that? After meditating for days I was in my office on a stinking hot summer day. I didn't want to move until I had nailed this. As I was sitting there, at least eight hours into my day, I picked up a book on my coffee table and opened casually on a page. There I saw the mandala of consciousness. For some reason that's when all of this fell into place. I could see that the Self, what we want, was in the middle of these four concentric circles and the basis of all mandalas was who I really am. Yet as a physical being I was outside of those circles; I was so separate. The things that weren't working for me in my world were happening because in that particular area I felt disconnected to who I really was. I just needed to devise a system to get from the contraction to the want – or what I call the A list, our true soul's want.

The beauty of working with what our soul wants is we start to become one with divine will, or Iccha, which is the Sanskrit word for pure will. It's a different intention, a different feeling, and the results are different. Divine will is inspiration. It's expansion, it's all-inclusive, and it's loving and insightful. Divine will pulls you along. Meanwhile, our will, which we sometimes mistake as divine will, is dominating. It's controlling, manipulative, proud, arrogant, stubborn and insecure. Divine will is pure consciousness. It flows through us as beings of consciousness.

Whatever consciousness is, and whatever the inherent qualities of consciousness are, that is exactly who we are. How comforting is that? They're the only things we need to find, to remember. For a She-Monk, this brings out her best qualities because this is being the I AM. It is being purely her, living creatively. This is nurturing; this is the path of least resistance. It fully centres us in life in a lovely way. We're so focused and we're so devotional. All our problems and all the little things that would previously hook us in go behind us; we don't see them as often anymore.

This creates freedom and possibility, allowing us to create our own divine story. It is also a very easy way to help someone see if they have been in a tough time, that they're actually having a tantrum. Most of my work is showing disgruntled or upset people that they're having a tantrum. Once their ego accepts that they've just had a tantrum, the person will usually laugh – even if they've been through something quite upsetting. A tantrum simply means that we've experienced something we don't want.

One problem area that was of interest to me was merging my spiritual side with my other love: personal development. Although there was some overlap they were fundamentally different and I found it difficult to merge them. I preferred to come from love and devotion. Interestingly, I've found that people who get really into good-quality personal development can end up discovering grace, but they are rare. This is because we've never really been able to find who we mystically, originally are and live and function in the world at the same time. The day I randomly opened a book and saw the mandala was when I discovered how it all fell into shape. I could follow what I want and use the work I already knew by working with language, feeling, action and visualisations. When looking at a mandala you can see that we have pure self (the dead centre). We then manifest this into an energy form of emotion and pure will. This is feeling. Then, on the next stage of manifestation, we become thought and intuition, and then on the next stage we become the body and action. Outside of the circles is the gross experience of being a human being.

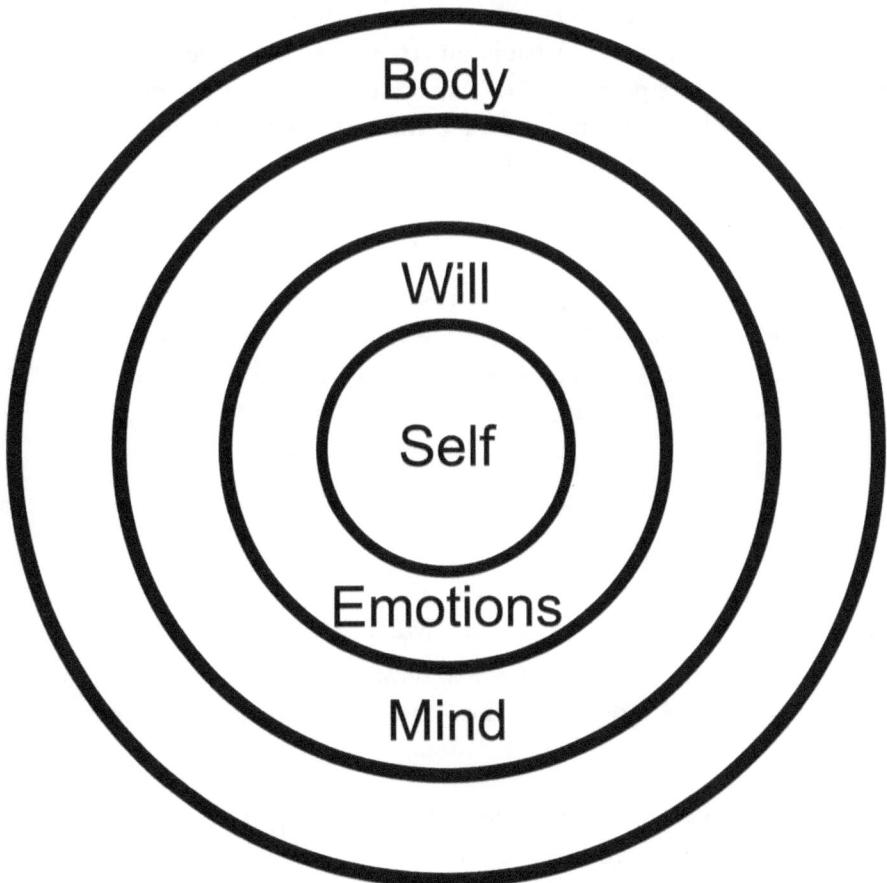

By becoming intelligent about our wants, we take care of the different levels that we need to integrate. These include the senses, our thoughts – which are our belief systems – the language we use and our emotions, which originally are love, joy, happiness, peace.

If something is off, it's very easy to see the corresponding work that needs to be done. In my tradition, these are called upayas, the pathway, steps back to freedom.

If you want to heal and find the break in the story, then sit down and say to yourself, "Okay, I know who I've been and I accept what I've been doing. Now what the hell is it that I want?" I put them into two categories: the A and B lists. The A list is all the attributes of God, of consciousness that we are, like peace, joy, happiness, wisdom, oneness, beauty, love, etc. The B list is more what we think we want coming from separation and need, like material things, change, or the wish to be in control. The A list is our real desire; the B list comes from a complaint and something outside ourselves. It's easier to start with the complaint or B list. Remember: the A list is our eternal self and we can expect it. The B list involves getting rid of expectations, as they are not what we really want and are causing suffering. Identify the B then enquire to the A. Find the real want then go for it with everything you have.

> 'Magic is when you use your mind to tell the universe what you want it to do for you. Miracles happen when you ask how you can be of service to the universe.'
> **– Marianne Williamson**

What we most want is what the universe wants for us. They are completely the same, in alignment. We never have to worry if we're in the Tao or universal flow if we're reminding ourselves every day of that thing that we most want: the beauty, the harmony, the love, and the communion.

So what did I want with my partner? I was looking at love from a needs place. I wanted love, to be love and to be loved by him. I thought I'd found someone who could be on the same page with me and we could be love together. However, there was an unconscious expectation that caused me suffering. When I saw it was simply straight up *love* that I wanted I cried. Many people do this when they get in touch with the pain of separation. I wasn't being the I AM in the world; I was being the I AM only with myself and then sliding into something else as soon as difficulty arose. My heart wanted to be in love all the time with consciousness and the universe tried to tell me this through my situation.

I love watching clients have this breakthrough. They realise they are behaving a certain way because they want peace, harmony, abundance, wellbeing, freedom. I will talk more about this later but what a boon it is to work out that's all it is and to sit with the peace that comes from the recognition of who we really are.

## What if I want my partner to change?

That's a B want, a no deal. You have to give that up. This is the beauty of being a She-Monk. The practice is tied up in the relationship situation. You have to accept them. You have to hold the space for them to be and know who they are and then lovingly enquire and guide them to what they want. Your stuff is always for you and it's all about you; it's never about the other. The same is true for them. What we want in another is usually a reflection of what we want in ourselves. This means we are coming from a place of separation. If it's a serious issue, then you need to get help with it. If your partner is abusive or distant or depressed, get them help. If they can't get help, get help yourself to see what you can do. Remember that it's their stuff. Know what you want and be really proactive with it. When you know what you want you automatically create spaciousness and you take the hook, the expectation, out of that other person. This eases the pressure, allowing your relationship to flourish. Be honest and know what you want. It's not always going to be nice at first. You're going to face humiliation because you're going to change some of the things that you've been doing.

There will be things that you haven't owned or looked at, but this is the ultimate experience and is very healing.

## What if I can't work out what I want?

You just need some help. Try my wants meditation on my website (www.sallythurley.com/meditations) where I run a list of divine qualities by people to see where their complaint fits. For example, say someone really dislikes where they live and they want a new home. The issue really could be of abundance. They may want money to be able to afford their dream home and so they'll do what they need to do to make it beautiful. Often hearing the word 'abundance' triggers an emotion within them. I'll then expand them and their vision through what I call a Spanda Mandala, creating space for abundance to come.

A belief could also be in the way, or maybe you really don't want to see it. Maybe you believe it's beneficial to be caught up in the drama, the story, the trauma or the tantrum. You may be overwhelmed. Anxiety and stress are symptoms of being overwhelmed and occur when we don't know what we want, when we have too many options or when we haven't done the work. It's very emotional discovering what you knew already deep down inside. To be given permission to go for what you already are. How wonderful if every parent did this for their kids! I'm so used to it now I can read what people want in their energy and then can help bring in the vision, the feeling, the action of what they want. My kids, in particular. You must use my mandala, download the exercise and do it all the time to see why you are struggling in this situation, and to purify your wants and take them home.

## What if I don't believe I can have it?

That's the ego talking. This is very common. Not only can you have it, you already do, you are it! That's the joke, the irony. When you realise what you already have and use it to inspire you, then you start living divinely. You're coming from your Self in every action. At the end of the day we are happily committed, determined spiritual beings, which will be enough inspiration to move around the resistance that comes up. The ego wants to hold on. That's its job. Blow it a kiss and say, "Thanks, but I'm moving on." It comes back to delicious things like trust, faith, living with uncertainty and letting grace lead the way. Try it on. Knowing your heart's desire and soul's calling is a big game-changer. It's the best skill you can have and gift to another. If you let those around you know your highest want, then they can help, guide, motivate and inspire you. It will be also inspiring to them. The ultimate win-win.

The spanda mandala method is so simple and a lot of fun. I wanted something that was easy to do anywhere and anyhow, and I also like things that get me physically active. This method came from that day I was in so much pain and agony that I wasn't going to move until I sorted it out. When I saw the mandala it fell into place for me. It's a science on its own, an old science of consciousness that I've tweaked to help people discover their heart's desires. I run regular workshops in this and give private sessions. You will find the details on my website.

The best way to get from a B list to an A list is to look at the complaint. "I'm miserable." Why are you miserable? "I'm miserable because I'm not a success." So what do you want? "I want to be a success." Well, that's an ego thing, because we all want to be recognised, loved, and seen as something in the world. So why do you want the feeling of being a success? "When I'm successful I'm proud of myself. When I'm successful I know I've achieved something. When I'm successful I'm happy." So then you can say because happy is who you are. Do you want to be happy? That's it. That's your A list. "I want to be happy." See how it makes everything fall into place. It's so uplifting too, isn't it? Recognise that suffering is a tantrum, no matter the size. We are rejecting our present moment, whether in grief or whether we are reacting to a slight and pulling away love. Seeing what I really want in the moment always brings me back to a laugh and lightens the mood and for me it snaps me out of my tantrum. These questions are all that matters: "What do I want and what am I doing to get it?" Yep, you take action, the inspired kind.

It's really healing to say you're having a tantrum. Admit you're pushing away a situation that you really don't want. It may have been something horrendous and so your reaction would seem justified. But in time you'll start to see differently with the work, the divine plan action. If you don't like an outcome, check what your expectations have been and move them up a level. By this I mean, move it to your A list. Find that quality of the Self that you already are, the one you wish to see and manifest more of in the world.

*Chapter four*

# YOUR MANIFESTO

Commitment, I found, is the key to putting your knowledge of what you want into action and receiving it. It takes perseverance, determination, forbearance and it's where the rubber hits the road. This is truly where we become a She-Monk. We make a manifesto! Here we take the teachings, the inspiration and we make it our own by choice and a dedication to a highest good and those around us.

Once we turn the want into a personal commitment or manifesto, we create the daily path to getting through any situation. It is the beginning of the roadmap home while in the world and it is handy in every single moment. It also teaches us how to deal with fear and old patterns.

This is where we put a stake in the ground and say, "This is what I want! This is who I am and who I'm going to be in every situation and every moment." There is nothing easy about this. This is all theory unless you put it into practice. Very few people will take it the whole way. As soon as we encounter something difficult, we drop it, our dedication. We freak out, say it doesn't work and we run away.

When we make a manifesto and commit we're showing the universe our resolve, and when we make a resolve the universe meets us. I remember hearing once a Hare Krishna saying if you take one step towards God, God will take five steps towards you. I love this because it's not just meeting us with one step, God is gushing towards us; it shows the nature of the divine, magnanimous and generous. Make the right move and dance with the universe.

At a personal development course I did once, called Landmark, I learnt that you cannot break a commitment. You can only break a promise. How cool is that? I found this compassionate and relieving. It's like the analogy 'if you fall off a horse, you jump straight back on'. You can't fail; there is no right or wrong. You're pursuing going home. You're pursuing what your heart desires, what your soul desires and most needs, which takes great patience. This will teach you the virtue of patience.

Going through this I really learnt what it means to 'have the patience of a saint'. As soon as you start to treat a situation differently and bring light, awareness and spirit to it, people react. Really react, like the wicked witch of the west in *The Wizard of Oz*. 'Oh, I'm melting!' Becoming the light can be too much for some and the temptation to want to pull out of the temporary chaos and rejection is huge. Hang in there. Stuff is about to sort out and change. It takes a level of trust in the universe.

I discovered in my journey doing spiritual work that many spiritual people stay only with the practice. What I mean is they go onto the yoga mat where they do their practice. When it's meditation time, they sit in meditation. They go somewhere and listen to singing bowls. They'll read the theory, the scriptures, they'll learn philosophy and then, after that act, it's all for them and off they go back into the world. They leave the spirituality on the mat. They leave the meditation in the room.

It's sad to see some spiritual people not integrating their spirituality into their life. Sometimes they are caught up in personal development, in the world of success and ambition. They think this is realer and that it overrides the woo-woo of spirituality. Or else they become boastful and arrogant and hide behind it.

After we get the experience of the divine and the cosmic downloads from our practice it's actually meaningless unless we put them into conscious action. This takes commitment. It's the path to right living and a happy life. You need to reassess your wants and put them into action and, as time goes on, you reassess, you go back, you do your mandala and you make a new manifesto.

> 'Your life changes the moment you make a new, congruent and committed decision.'
> **– Tony Robbins**

When we don't do this, we discover that we are all theory and no transformation, no action. This can happen all too often in the spiritual arenas, so we hide behind our cards and crystals, our uniforms and diets, and we don't make the big changes.

We wear beads, we wear white, we wear robes and yet we're not sincerely being what they really represent in the world. We can get stuck in the effort of all this uniform wearing too, in the trying to be seen to be doing and saying the right thing but it's not congruent in us yet. It's a push and controlling of ourselves and others, willing against the universe. This means that we're out of flow with the Tao. When we don't have the commitment we don't have the most important thing we need to pull off this delicate, raw, humbling process. When we don't have the commitment we can be uninspired and uninspiring. Often without that stake in the ground, we become lost in the dark and, when negative things happen to us, we give up our faith and practice. We become prone to perceiving our efforts as failures and thinking we're not good enough. These awful thoughts start to bombard us. I know because I go there too.

Sometimes we might not be sick enough of our situation so it continues. We might have a high tolerance level to what is happening. But remember: what we tolerate, we create. We could have co-dependency tendencies and not know it. We wait for a crisis point instead of taking life by the reins.

Maybe you don't yet have a vision that you believe in enough. You haven't sat in the feeling of what you want and what is being called through you. You haven't felt that deep emotional connection to the mystical, the one that almost makes you cry, it's so sweet. Tears will come when you get in touch with what your soul wants. When we don't commit to being the best us, or if we don't stick at it, we're saying to spirit, "I'm not worthy!" This defies self-love.

Here we are talking again about self-love. After accepting who we are, the greatest act of self-love we can perform is to put our highest value first and create from it. Sticking with the manifesto indicates to us the work that needs to be done; it shows where our strengths and weaknesses lie. There'll be times when we can't always pull it off, the commitment, and yet this is simply reflecting that there are things in us that are unhealed. It also shows us where to put our efforts and attention.

Sometimes we are unable to commit because we are holding on to something we need to release. We might need to adjust our beliefs and mindset. Sometimes we need to use new language to change our neural pathways and help our nervous system.

Once we make a manifesto, we have something we can actually engage with and use in a really straightforward way. Life and karma are all about choice. Choice is the only part that is free will. The rest is God's will. Poor choices take us away from the Self; good choices take us closer. The commitment is the golden thread that keeps us dedicated. It prevents us from going down with the story, the meaning of disaster, the trauma, the failure and it gives us aligned, good choices.

When I work with people I find they have fun doing their mandala, finding acceptance and having big breakthroughs. At this stage they are really inspired, but after a week or so they tend to zone out or give up. They find it too confronting. So many people want to be enlightened straight away. They want an instant fix and are too scared of the unknown, too scared to break free of what's not working for them. Spiritual practice or sadhana takes time.

When I discovered the mandala and put it into practice I found where I was far from perfect straight away. In fact, there were times when I would want to throw it out the window. Fortunately, it became a very inspirational, useful tool. I stuck to it and, to my delight and fascination, it did save the relationship, but not for long. I started to live out of a different heart space, started to see empowerment in a whole new way. I started to 'live and talk the yoga' and the universe showed the gap that was being *created* between me and my partner, who I loved dearly.

Things started to get really rough again. When I was disabled I could see that my partner wasn't with me in what was happening. I could see from the way he pulled away that we were going to hit the rocks. I made a decision one day and I thought, 'This is not going to be roadkill. This is not going to hit the wall. This is not going to fall out of the sky and crash everywhere. Somehow I'm going to keep my heart open because anything is better than closing my heart.' I've had a lot of trauma in my life. I've had enough opportunities, reasons and excuses to keep my heart closed, to blame situations. I know how awful that is, how much work it takes to open up again and admit what has happened.

This is where the manifesto came from. How do I be the best me possible with all this uncertainty? Let's be straight up here. I have a powerful personality and some big tendencies to overcome. I knew I had to have something huge to work with to anchor me through and keep a contract with myself and God is what it took. I'm not alone here, right? I had to move towards inspired action while holding myself together and keeping my spiritual centre. So I created my manifesto – a pledge or contract between myself and God. It was challenging. I was dealing with a suite of massive life-changing issues at the time. Sometimes my partner and I would interact and I would hold my new resolve. I would behave very well. I'd be loving and self-loving, which was a new thing for me. Big time. So I'd say, "I don't think our relationship is going somewhere good right now. Can we change it?" And if that didn't work, if things went on as they were, I'd say, "Okay, I'm just letting you know that I'm going to remove myself to be able to explore a new way of doing this."

To my surprise this made him angrier and angrier. Sometimes he would needle at me until I exploded. If I did lose it, I'd think, 'Okay, what did I do? How can I go back to being love?' At the time, I thought I wanted a relationship. In fact, my entire life that's what I dreamt of. What a huge pressure for a partner! Goodness! I mean, I was married by twenty-one. I was going to get it right and I was determined to have what my grandparents and few others had and finally get that closeness I craved as a kid. But what I really wanted was love, just love – to be and love myself and be loved by God. I had to go through this process. My relationship was the perfect training ground. Even though we didn't work out, he was the best partner for me at the time and I learnt so much. I have nothing but love and gratitude for him.

It was a volatile time. We had a lot around us going wrong and some days I just knew I didn't have what it took to be all the things I was inspired to be. I'd say, "Manifesto, I can't do you today. I just can't. I'm in too much pain, I'm too unwell, and I'm too tired." At least I was conscious of that. I knew that I wasn't going to pull it off, but I kept my commitment to be the She-Monk, to crack the code, without getting too sucked into the world and without hiding behind my spirituality. That was the imperative part. Acknowledging this helped me heal too. It was part of acceptance.

It's funny, because this seems very much like what people do in straightforward personal development. The difference is we're aligning with our soul's want. I knew many old yogis, spiritual practitioners and healers who went to places like India or Tibet when the East was opening up to the West. They'd done a lot of sadhana or spiritual work and were often very proud of this. There were some at the ashram. I observed that many of them were quite dysfunctional. Once they left India, or Tibet, or their ashram they completely fell apart. This may have been because the magic was gone. Some walked away and became hard. Many didn't know what to do next. They didn't realise that they had more to do, another step. When something is taken from you it's actually a sign that you are ready to move onto something else. I was lucky because I had my centre for twenty years. When it left my life it was time – in fact, it was overtime – to move on, which was quite challenging and painful. It was, however, the perfect opportunity to nut this out because I'm not on my own here; there are many of us wanting to hold onto that experience and be in the world.

I found that many of these old yogis were hiding behind their spiritual experiences. They would be bragging all the time, saying, "Oh, well in our day we would do this and we would do that, and it was so much more powerful with X, Y, Z ..." I'd look at them and they'd be a complete mess. Their vibe and walk didn't match their talk. They weren't congruent with what they were saying and in the end I didn't even really care about what they were saying. I mean, who really cares about your stories of dancing with the divine if your life is completely in turmoil or you're hard? Hint here: the story is nothing; it's what you do with it! Have you claimed your life or are you stuck in the past? What needs to happen here?

I'm not saying you're going to pull this off straight away and you're going to be great at it. It is a lifetime's work. I admit that. I'm always discovering something new. This requires a lot of mastery and it might not even happen in this life. I have a feeling it might if you really stick to it, but this is a way to happiness and fulfilment in this life regardless. This work needs to be done. It simply requires commitment. These are the strides we need to take to be out in the world, but not of it. This can be the most painful part of this whole experience. It's quite frightening. Knowing and accepting who you are is the meat of the work.

I came to a crunch point with my partner. Something took place and I saw finally that I could be making headway; I could do this. It made me see I was now living the calling; spirit and I were working together. We took the children and went on a holiday to Bali at the worst possible time and it just burst. It all exploded. We were literally there one day and everything instantly deteriorated. It was clear there was no coming out of it. I was very ill at that stage. We literally decided in forty-eight hours that it was over. We were breaking up. Again.

After the initial pain, it surprisingly didn't take long for me to reach to what was louder for me. "Use this situation, girl. Break old patterns. Be who you want to be through this." My inner dignity presented itself through the pain and negative behaviour we had thrown at each other. I heard my authentic self say, "Okay, this is what this situation is for. This is why we do this work. This is what the manifesto and the mandala is all about: getting through the best way possible and learning and growing from it."

The relationship was the impetus to find the technology I ended up using when really it was more my desire to be a strong and independent spiritual woman who embraced the world and wasn't made small by any and all old traditional paradigms. I saw how much of a trap it is to not be able to own each and every moment of who we are. Fess up: do you behave like a saint in each and every moment? Of course not. I personally doubt anyone does. What if we could change this to being committed to what we want in that moment?

When we got home we discovered the ashram community we'd been a part of had also split apart. We lost most of our friends overnight and I knew that I was going to have to move homes while still disabled and quite sick. This was going to be an ongoing process to get through.

From the extraordinary presence and grace that came from my holiday experience, because I was keeping my heart open and committed to it,

I knew that the universe would give me everything I needed. There was no doubt. I felt totally loved and supported. It would give me the right home, the right situation, the right financial setup and it did. I didn't have to do a thing. All I had to do was make sure that I did this work. This is the work of budding She-Monks. This is She-Monk mastery. It's fabulous!

> 'Your task is not to seek for love, but merely to seek and find all the barriers within yourself you have built against it.'
> **– Rumi**

The manifesto is for everyone. It is the attention and directing of Self and consciousness to the highest good in everyday events and with all the people we come across. Here we use the world as our mirror, our playground for transformation. It doesn't matter if it's our partner, children, bosses, work colleagues or the person down the street, the lady in the chemist. It's our commitment to being and in all situations what we most want.

Here is the manifesto below. This is all I stuck to. The first line is enough. In the beginning that is all I had. I then added other things that came up, as they covered other areas. Basically, you must know what you want on a soul level then commit your life to being it. When that no longer works then maybe there's a new want it's time to go over this process again. The beauty is that no matter what you choose as your A list soul want it will work because remember they are all attributes of who you really are, of God. It's a win-win situation! If you stick to it. Also remember, you can't break it. We all fall off. You simply learn from the experience to jump back on the horse and clean up the mess you made.

Make a copy of this manifesto and fill in the gaps. Make it a beautiful contract and put it on your wall. Put it where you can easily access it. Feel free to amend it to include what is really important to you.

This totally changed my life. I needed something so concrete and took it on as a holy vow. It moved from theory and talk and put the onus directly on to me to be the love and transformation in my life. This was my stake in the ground for consciousness to stick to and support and it did, in every way.

> I, ..................,
>
> Am committed to my heart's desire, my soul's want: ....................

**This is my personal commitment to myself.**

- I understand that I can never break a commitment. If I forget or mess it up, I will simply read this, remember what I stand for and start again in the present moment.

- I am no longer a victim, hopeless or lost.

- I know having the right perspective is the path to hope.

- I take *full* responsibility for my world, my thoughts, my actions and my feelings.

- I fully accept my light and my dark.

- I accept and allow everything that flows through me as my experience.

- I know everything is a play of consciousness.

- I do daily spiritual practices of ..................... (list at least three).

- I regularly sit in communion with spirit and listen to divine guidance.

- I inquire what is truth in each moment.

- I give others the space to be themselves and to grow and evolve as they need.

- I give up handing my power to others.

- I give up controlling or dominating.

- When I am lost or suffering I remember that I am .................... and ask my highest self what do I need to do in this moment to be that.

- I always check in and see if what I am doing or choosing is congruent to self-love.

- I excuse myself from all previous expectations to be anything other than my pure free natural self.

- I remember that I can either change a situation, accept it or leave it.

- The activities that best bring me back to the Self are: ....................... (list at least three)

- I always forgive.

- I come from nothing.

- I love.

- I live my vision and heal my life and bring peace to the world.

## To me, commitment sounds hard.

Well, you need a new perspective and to clean up what the word commitment means to you. Alternatively, you can find another word that means the same thing. See it simply as the life buoy, the lifeline that shows you what to do when you most need help. Remember a commitment cannot be broken. It's malleable and flexible. It's not about rules. It's a pledge to yourself. It's ultimate self-love and your way out of pain and suffering. It's only between you and yourself. If you beat yourself up and are scared of the commitment, then investigate your language and beliefs. They're not serving you. Just see this as an experiment and take it on, even if for only a week. If you can't do it because you don't like the sound of commitment, then ask yourself what can you imagine would work for you, to be that free liberated soul in the world?

## What if I didn't get to the right want?

If it's an attribute of your highest self, then it's what you want. It might not be the exact one straight away, but they're all in the same family; they're all love, all God. Whichever one you pick it will work and help get you closer as you experiment. Remember it's in the doing that we learn and sort things out. You can't fail. If you want more beauty, wellbeing and abundance, follow love. Put that as your want. Put 'To be home, communion, peace' and see what happens. Do the meditation again. It may be clearer this time.

## I don't think I can make it work.

Well, did you get help? This is not easy work. It is difficult. I had many upsets in my life. There was a lot to overcome. Even in my background training and attainment, there came a point where I needed someone to talk regularly to keep me on track. Sometimes we clearly see what we've been doing, what has been coming up for us and what tendencies we've been running from, how manipulative we've been without even knowing it. We think we can't face humiliation. We don't like to be wrong. We're really always thinking for ourselves. We're always being selfish, even if we think we give everything up for another. Why do we do that? Is it not to get something in return?

I had a lot of fight in me because of my background. I was so afraid of being controlled and in pain that I'd either run from it or fight it. Naturally, I always managed to find controlling partners. I had unhealed personal and karmic stuff, and in some cases I had the wrong perspective. I have to say this was partly due to my spiritual background. I was taught that what was best for me personally, my role was to fully surrender my being, power, desires and goals to my partner. To have little ambition and to be fully there for them and in my earnestness I did it. That advice got me into a worse place. It was such a disaster. I know this advice contributed to the relationship struggles and I'd stay sick and lethargic as long as it was like that. Every part of my being fought with me as I tried to nut out this relationship thing. Anyone living out something like that, please … stop now.

The manifesto helped me see what was first and foremost self-love. If what I was doing was feeling at odds with being what I most wanted (e.g. say I wanted to be wise but was doing something unwise) then I would scrap it and meditate. I would ask God, "What do you want me to do in this situation? I want to be wisdom and yet I don't know how it's going to play out right now." The answer will always come and will come without you even trying. You can say to your partner, "I really want to be wise right now. I can't access the inspiration or the words. Can you help me?" And all you can do is hope and pray that they're going to be wise and loving enough to see how sincere and authentic you are being.

The best breakthrough for me was in how I was with my children. All of this process was designed to keep an intimate relationship. Fascinating how the relationship went and yet it brought my children and I closer together. We have a magnificent, harmonious relationship and they are teenagers! I was so authentic and sincere in all my communication with them that they easily met that energy. Life has consequently become so gorgeous with them.

## Actions:

Make this your creative project. Put your manifesto up. Treat it like it's a pledge. Make it artistic. Frame it. Originally, I had some old-fashioned kind of agreement in mind, written in inked script and a red seal, but that's the romantic in me. I now have it drawn up on sketch paper and love it. Let others see it, have it on show. It takes strength to be so open like this. Don't worry about what others think or being humiliated. When you're going down this path, humiliation is one of the things we have to deal with. It helps free us.

## Give the manifesto to another.

Another action step is to find a friend who wants the same as you, another She-Monk. Check in with each other. Find out what's been difficult? What do you need to shed some light on? What did you fail at? What was hard? What was getting in the way? How can you congratulate yourself? What can you appreciate? Can you feel love? Can you feel love becoming the dominant energy in the world? Are your relationships in harmony? Have the wrong energies finally left you? What space can you see that you've created? How's your world improved? What has been taken away? What is no longer a match to who you are?

Celebrate! This is the hard stuff. This is love in action. This is what will transform you. This is what will give you the grace you long for.

## Chapter five

# SOUL CALLING

We are doing all this inquiring, investigation, practicing and journeying because we want the best life ever. We want it to be from a connected and enlightened space. We're spiritual and life rebels. It is possible to have the best of both worlds. We want to be able to find a way to live by our skills, our gifts, our passions and what lights us up. What we have can be of service and God is the boss. When we do this, life elegantly falls into place and it happens when we follow our soul's calling, our heart's desire, our purpose for being or, in other words, our dharma.

When we switch to wanting to live by our own rules, ignoring what society thinks is right or wrong, or what job our parents think we should have, or which career we should get funnelled into, we become aware and listen more to our intuition. We tap into what consciousness wants us to do.

We start to listen to our intuitive being. We live from pure will, that 'iccha' I explained before. This pure will is also pure love and is a precursor to pure action. They are one and the same and they are here to help us. They are running through each and every one of us as universal love and support. Living our soul's purpose makes us radically appreciative of everything, even what has happened to us in the past.

We start to see that no matter how awful or wonderful the situations in our life have been, they've been there because they've helped us get to where we are now. They've given us glimpses and signs of what is underneath and behind our pain, bodies, fears, worries and expectations. Everything suddenly links. We end up happy. Purpose makes us happy and we cannot wait to start the day. I'm amazed that I've become a Monday morning lover.

You breathing? You have a purpose. This isn't about fame and fortune. Far from it, it can be subtle and private and unique to you but it is there nonetheless. Often it requires investigating outside of the box and it is usually right under your nose. So fascinating!

When I was in the 'normal' mode of living I thought there was something wrong with me. None of it made sense. School was a grind, having a nine to five job was a grind. Even though I thought they were what I was meant to be doing, inside I was screaming *"Are you kidding me?"* I'd get these jobs because that's what we do. You grow up, get educated and you get a job. But I was miserable. Mondays were the worst day and Friday afternoons were what I lived for.

But now I live for Monday morning because it signifies creation and playtime. Seriously. Sunday's an important inner-world day. Usually by Sunday afternoon I have ideas and inspiration pouring through me. I'm excited for Monday morning where I'm up, vigorous and jumping to start my day. That is what living with purpose is like.

Another beautiful aspect of living like this is that we own our zone of genius. There is a great quote that says: "Everybody is a genius. But if you judge a fish by its ability to climb a tree, it will live its whole life believing that it is stupid."

When we're living in this zone of purpose, we become aware of our innate genius. Guess what? You have a genius. My guess is it's something you take totally for granted or maybe you are terrified of it so it doesn't get much airtime, if any at all. The greatest potential for our purpose is to take our love, knowledge and healing to the world and help others. This is because it's all wrapped up in our genius, in our service to the world. We are being servants of spirit.

When we live our purpose, we become magnets for grace. Consciousness is attracted to people who are living for their heart's desire and soul's purpose. No longer do we have to do everything, take on board all the things we 'should' do because we realise the sweetness of bringing it all into one. In Sanskrit they called this 'rasa' or 'nectar'. Find that thing and go for it with everything we have. Learning to let go of the outcome is, of course, a big part of being a She-Monk. That's a big part of being a yogi. This is living, journeying. Who obsesses now about an outcome when the journey is so alive and exhilarating?

If you want to do this, throw yourself into your purpose with no idea of where it's going. You don't even need to care; simply let yourself be alive. It makes you want to live. It makes you want to inspire everyone else around you to live. Get onto your purpose!

> 'Did you know that people who know why they wake up in the morning live up to seven years longer than those who don't?'
> **– Dan Buettner**

Our purpose is here and is why we're even alive. At some stage God thought 'Hmm, it's getting a bit boring being here, being a God and not knowing what it's like to enjoy standing on the outside looking in. It may be a fun idea to create something outside of myself, a universe maybe with creatures in it that have the capacity to remember who they are and come home. I'll create duality.' God continued, 'I don't know what it's like to experience myself' and through pure will, through pure knowledge and action, the universe was created along with our reason for being. We experience ourselves through our interaction with the world. This gives us clues of our true nature and origin. It starts with the five senses, what we can perceive and what actions we can perform, and then moves beyond for those who take on meditation, prayer and practices like that, doing what consciousness wishes for us to do. Kind of a *Truman Show* in a way. Who needs murder mysteries on TV when the greatest mystery is Who am I?

Let's think of what it's like when we're not living purposefully. Without purpose, we are at the mercy and whim of others. We're not living our life; we're living a life that's been dictated to us, either by our parents, or by our teachers, by employees, or by our communities. That's not living. It's a helpful start, a blueprint we can launch from. If we ignore it, we in essence become disempowered. We are filling in, fitting in and, if you're a bit of a rebel like me, you know there's something more out there. You want to be free. Do you wake up on a Monday morning and it's just a drag? Are you in the rat race and wondering 'What on Earth am I doing with my life? I want more. I want more colour. How come she has more colour? How come she's doing really well and got this and that?' If you're thinking all that then you know you're not fully in your purpose. All this falls away when we live our purpose.

We're not sheep. Sheep are sheep. And yet we have this sheep mentality where we see how someone else is popular, or see them do something really well, and we come to believe that we have to do what they're doing. Or worse: we tell ourselves that they're special, different or lucky and that the results they've achieved are not for us.

When we ignore purpose we become closed off from our full intuition. When we're not living our purpose, we're not healing. Pause there for a moment. Can you sit with this? We don't heal without it. My healing crisis had me crack open so the purpose could show itself. When it did, I realised I wanted it all along.

The crazy thing was that even with all the work I'd done with teachers, mentors and spiritual communities, I was never – not in my whole time at the ashram – encouraged to find my purpose and do it with everything I had. If anything I was told, "Do your service here and that will give you all you need." No, it gave me a lot and seva is important, but it was out of balance and contributed to my crash. Then the cardinal sin was to heed the calling and take your spirituality to the world. Anything that stops you doing that is not spirituality; it's a very, very limited point of view. It's a myth. It's control. It's small. It's far more empowering to encourage people to trust their guts, go for what is being called and to learn to find their heart's desire and soul's calling, to totally support them and be there for them. That's the role of a spiritual mentor. That's what I am. I'm here to support you here and it's the best job ever. I was actually dying inside with all this experience.

My intuition was coming fast and strong. It was telling a different story to what I knew. I'd been on a pilgrimage to India a couple of times and I'd had very big experiences. One of them was during a very long early meditation. I was told clearly what the highest thing for me was, what God's vision of me was. I was also told that I wasn't putting my new awareness of what I am meant to be doing into action when I came home because I was too busy fitting in. I was fitting into the ashram's expectations, my partner's expectations and not knowing really what mine were. I simply bookmarked this as a nice and informative experience. This was a sign of a disempowered girl and I can only blame myself. That's why I had my healing crisis, my big, mystical universal experience. It was to radically shake me up because I had a mission here on this world. It had nothing to do with my little me so I had to shake my attachment to what I thought was the right way. The voice would speak loudly to me many times until I really listened. Our purpose is not about ourselves. We may have to learn things. For example, I have to learn to speak up, learn to be seen and learn to put myself out there in spite of criticism. These are all things I don't personally like and yet I'm here doing it. I'm here to do something. I'm here to help people break free and find that gorgeousness that is being themselves in the world. I'm here to simply be a She-Monk and help others do the same.

Another difficult aspect of not living our purpose is we become very mentally stuck. We start to judge, compare and measure. It's enough to work out how to get around the doubt and fear of our own limitations let alone what others think. When we're stuck in our heads we become cynical, fearful and judgemental of others. You know you're off track when getting sucked into this. Sometimes deep down we become jealous when we see other people living their purpose and having a fantastic experience of life. They know what they want while we're sitting there judging inwardly, saying, "I don't know what I want. It's all crap." How about this one: "There is no purpose in life other than to wake up and breathe." That's the sign of a cynic. A cynic has a blocked heart and doesn't realise that they are experiencing God. They're experiencing magic and experiencing the mystical already in every moment. They just have to get over themselves and feel it. But they're closed off and will honestly only get it and believe God is with them when some magical creature comes down from the skies.

If we're not living our purpose, we don't know what we're really capable of. Because once we're living in the Tao (flow with spirit), once we're doing our dharma, we start digging deep in areas that we had no idea existed within us.

> 'Everyone has a path. If you have life you have a purpose.'
> **– Carolyn Myss**

It's that simple. I found that before my purpose I was already ageing. Now my purpose is anti-ageing. There you go, girls. There's a good reason for it ;-) It is incredible how life-affirming your dharma is. And your dharma can be for anything. We're not all here to be Tony Robbins or Bill Gates, or some famous Olympic swimmer; we're meant to be who we're meant to be. Your dharma, or true place and duty in this world, might be to run an animal sanctuary. It might be to farm bees, do organic gardening, to teach kids with special needs, to run a multinational company that supports fair trade, to teach meditation like me or to work in palliative care and give dying people comfort.

At the end of the day our purpose is always I AM, to go to the I AM. We work with that which is flowing through us. It's not necessarily to be an entrepreneurial business magnate; it is simply about I AM. Chasing success can be an addiction. Sometimes it's a racket – something we do to fit in with society. We hide behind it and use it to create reasons why we don't step up to our calling. Happiness and wellbeing are wrapped up in our reasons for being and give us fulfilment.

When we discover that we're particularly good at something, that we have a genius, the natural impulse is to want to share it with others. We become expanded and joyous, which are infectious qualities. Giving, participating and loving the fact that there is something we are good at – even if it's just hugging our grandchildren and giving them a strong sense of self-worth – is some of the best work ever. It doesn't have to be our day job. Some people's calling may be voluntary work. Their day job may just be the means to the end. Therefore, we worship and praise the day job, seeing it as part of the service to the world.

But it is possible, if you're creative, to combine the two. You can do it and I have. The beauty of living your purpose is that you're involving all your centres of being – the physical, emotional and mental.

I interviewed a fellow entrepreneur recently – a Dutch lady who had spent some time in a nun monastery in Tibet. She was telling me that people in this culture know that unless you live your life purpose you become a zombie and that the majority of the people in the world are, in fact, zombies. If they're nuns it's because it was their purpose to be a nun. They're not confined or restricted by what their families say they have to do. They are fully encouraged to work out what lights them up.

When I was doing my health coaching I came across what's called the Blue Zones. It was my favourite study and is something I've brought in to share with my clients and the people I work with. Dan Buettner's twenty-year study with *National Geographic* involved going to various hotspots in the world where groups of people lived the longest and healthiest lives. They're not the places you would think. I would have thought, 'Oh, well China certainly and India will pop up there', but they didn't. Not even did Tibet. It was places like Greece, Italy, and there was even a part of America, believe it or not. By interviewing these people, he determined it wasn't one thing they did that made them live longer and happier. It wasn't down to singly nutrition or their job, but each country did have something in common. The Okinawans' version of this was called the 'Ikigai', which means 'that which you wake up for'. These cultures know that this is a fundamental part of our life journey, a basic human need: to be excited, to be lit up every single day, to wake up looking forward to doing something that you love, that you are called to do. The purpose has encoded in it that which we need to overcome. This is why it's part of the She-Monk. It's part of our development and growth and completely aligns with living a congruent life with spirit.

It's another version of the manifesto. It's the manifesto also in action because we need it to make it work. Living our purpose creates a pull so we no longer have to push. Yes, there are going to be things to overcome that are difficult and take time, so purpose doesn't happen overnight. That's the beautiful thing: it's all about the journey. There will be huge learning curves along the way that make us. That's what makes us the teachers in the world because we have overcome and persevered due to inspiration.

An indicator of what your purpose is can be uncovered by your dreams. For many years, from a young child right up until only about three years ago, I'd have these dreams that, for the first thirty years of my life, were nightmares. I'd be on a stage talking to crowds of people and trying to run away. The further I ran the deeper underground the stage would be. I was always standing on stage talking to people, but because it hadn't happened yet I didn't know what I was communicating. For someone like me who doesn't like the limelight, who is particularly private and, believe it or not, shy, these dreams were traumatising. Interesting how it became my hope. Seriously. Eventually I soon saw that when I was coming to the end of my time with my spiritual community, that I would hear questions and answers and I would hear people's responses and a part of me was dying to answer but I couldn't. It became so strong that I couldn't be held back anymore. The more I was held back or put down – if I did speak up I'd get it out wrong, I'd be humiliated – the more a part of me was dying inside and knew I had to find another way.

It's fascinating how I ended up getting a thyroid condition the longer I put off communicating and contributing. It was very clear to me when I was meditating or seeing healers. They'd say there was a bird in my throat that was trying to sing. They told me it was time to sing and speak up from my Self experience, which was extremely difficult as I do not like putting myself out there. I'd rather work with other people and yet I'd been born with a leadership makeup ... When I face and acknowledge who I am I see that I am fundamentally a leader type who loves communicating and inspiring others. See, I didn't say it's always easy, but the pull is strong so you keep going.

I had to learn to face those fears and now in doing some on my own my thyroid condition is healing nicely. My purpose is all about communicating and speaking to groups of people about what I know most: the Self.

Have a look at what your dreams are and see the link. I now look back and can see that even at school I was the one who'd stand up to defend others or put my hand up to do drama even though it terrified me. When I was a spiritual wholefoods chef, people wanted me to do workshops. I'd sweat while doing them. It would be awkward, but then afterwards there was this bliss of speaking truth. It was all about truth; they were a front for me to talk about God. There's a very clear indicator in speaking up. I get high, I get inspired and I start saying things that I didn't know I even knew sometimes.

One of the workshops that I hold for people, usually at the beginning and middle of the year, is my spanda mandala life map workshop. This is a full-day workshop and involves doing the wants, the mandala and the manifesto. Then, at the end of the day, I help them create a painting, which becomes their life vision board. It's a beautiful work of art. One of the best outcomes for me was seeing a bookkeeper friend do the most magnificent painting, a painting that still, if I see it to this day, speaks radically of what she wants. Her life completely changed direction. I've never had a client come that hasn't reviewed what they're doing and saw a need to clean up and start making changes. The beautiful thing about having a painting mandala is that it's always there to remind them and take them back to that day when we worked together.

This friend of mine realised that she wanted freedom. That was her highest want. She was a great yogini and was brilliant with finances, so when she started focusing on and meditating on freedom, she saw that she actually didn't like working for clients the way she currently was. She didn't like having to do things in a never-ending cycle for other people and missing the link between money and spirit. A part of her was dying to stand up and own who she is and her amazing skills. She wanted to be independent in every possible way. She had the calling to be an entrepreneur; she just wasn't awake to it.

She ended up merging her skills. She found a way to merge her very creepy psychic, intuitive yogic relationship with money. We're talking about someone who, when she balances your books, actually gets a psychic download about your physical and mental health, your everything, and helps heal it. She's now using this concept as a business platform to become an entrepreneur. She's happier and has hope, vision and purpose.

When you are ready and open the purpose will just start. I wasn't ready because I didn't let it in, but you may be ahead of me. Funnily enough, though, you will see it's in the background already happening. The universe will create a window for you. You don't have to think about it too hard. The time will come when you will be given the opportunity. At the height of my illness and all that relationship stuff – literally within ten minutes of hearing that my community had torn apart – I launched a business. I knew the name and bought the domain. I set up a Facebook page and I started making quotes of hope and sharing them every single day. It flowed from me and, even with all that difficulty, I was happy and knew where I was going. Crazy.

It was fascinating how, in some kind of seed form, this desire to launch Spanda Living, my business came. It was just a no-brainer. I just did it because I was already doing it. I'd made my manifesto, I knew what I wanted and no trauma was large enough to make me a victim any more. No circumstances were going to dictate my life anymore. It was not going to be hard. No way; I refused to do it hard. On the surface it looked like it was hell. It was extremely stressful and my body responded like it was hell, but a deep part of me, the Self part, knew everything would be okay… I wasn't gripped by the trauma and the drama. I saw that this was the birthplace of my business and the best thing I ever did.

This was a push from the universe – and not just a little push. All those traumatic things were set up for me to jump off the cliff. It was a divine setup. It was radical. The universe wanted me to do this and I was ready. I was remarkably ready and very present. Have you come to the edge of a cliff? Have you been pushed off? Can you see a cliff coming? Do you realise this is a very exciting time that may be the making of you? What is the universe trying to tell you? What does it want you to know and do?

The Bhakti Sutras have a saying: 'Without desire pointing man's feet to the path of his duty … Let them show by example how work is holy when the heart of the worker is fixed on the highest.' This is a beautiful quote and reminds us that no matter what we're doing, we keep our focus on the highest. Our job might be our purpose. It may be our hobby or it could simply be motherhood. When I had my young babies I was feeling exhausted and flat. I remember a good friend saying to me, "It's your job right now; it's your purpose." I took this on like that and it completely transformed my experience. I put every single thing I had into being the best mother possible, with whatever limitations or skills that I had.

No matter what we're doing we're learning to honour, find love, worship and appreciate the work we are faced with. You don't have to quit your job if you're not ready, but if you're getting intel that it's time to quit your job and you don't do it the job will be taken away from you anyway. This is not always pretty, so instead of waiting to be pushed off a cliff and have everything taken from you like me, be brave enough to just jump. Hear the calling and go. Are you at a place where you know deep down inside that you can't do this another day? That's when we start turning our ship around towards our purpose, if we choose.

Be open. If it's your job, if it's to be a great partner, if it's to be a stay-at-home mum, if it's to be a taxi driver, it doesn't matter. If it's to become an entrepreneur, to setup a not-for-profit organisation, to save children from detention centres. That's fantastic.

Here's what I think: The purpose of life is wrapped up in why there is life. God has played a game where he created a way to forget Himself and then go on a journey of experiences to remember who He is. We are always playing that out. The discovery of the eternal moment is grace, recognising we are love and sharing that happiness with others using our talents and skills.

Here are some other questions to ponder and consider. For this exercise no answer is too silly, private, personal or crazy. Everything matters! Believe me. Holding back only holds you back and keeps treasures hidden deep inside so that we never get the joy of seeing them.

Let it *all* hang out. At the end, see what the common themes are and what makes you smile.

- What do you love to do most?
- What work do you do that doesn't feel like work (i.e. you could do it all day every day)?
- What do you do that makes you happy or content, even if you only do it for ten minutes?
- What are your unique abilities or gifts?
- What attributes do you have?
- What work do you do that brings you closer to the Self, to spirit?
- What do your friends, family and work colleagues say is your unique gift?
- What can we count on your for?
- If money was no object, what would you do?
- What makes you passionate? What cause that could help others gets you intense and 'vocal'?

- What are your professional skills and qualifications?
- Why do you think you are here?
- What came up for you in the wants, mandala exercises?
- What are your reoccurring dreams, beliefs, daydreams or fantasies?

If you would like to have fun putting it all together, use the Ikigai template. Simply draw on a large sheet of paper and write your main answers in each section under the appropriate heading. I use this when working out my services and offerings. It's fantastic.

## What if it turns out to be a mistake?

There is no mistake. Have a chat with me or your spiritual mentor. Find people who support you here. Your fear is talking. You want to jump, jump! Look at your issues of self-worth. Look at trust. The

She-Monk trusts the universe. Go deeper into communion. Living is when we don't really know for sure what is going to happen. We are simply in the moment. It's all about the present moment. There are no mistakes; the only option is to learn and embrace. We expand our being by learning and growing, but this first comes from the stillness. If you are earnest and sincere and spend time daily in communion with the present moment, with that eternal moment, the direction will come and challenge you. You'll have to overcome your own inhibitions and fears to be what the universe wants you to be. It can be a significant steppingstone. You don't know for some time what the outcome will be. Where am I going? Is this going to be worth it? But in the feeling of being alive and wanting to wake up you'll know that you are living your purpose. So embrace every step of the way. There is no mistake; there is only doing. And consciousness loves when we do on its behalf.

## How can you tell the right path from delusion?

You need to have an understanding of what is truth and have spent time doing self-enquiry. This is why I bang on about knowing who you are. The ego is cunning and will want to talk you out of this. I hear you too. Sometimes people get very deluded even following their calling because they stop the work, the practice. There are many deluded spiritual teachers out there – particularly teachers who think, 'Well, I'm perfect. Anything I do must be perfect', which is simply not true. Being a good person is a choice. So you have to be really, really honest. The ego wants to control. It wants fame, control and reassurance. It wants recognition and it's pushy. The calling, on the other hand, is a pull. It's inspiring. It can be scary at times, but you no longer give a damn. It's not about fame, but you might have to, like in my case, put yourself out there and be seen because how else will people know they can work with you?

Fame might be a part of your calling, but it doesn't mean that it is for everyone. It should not be the reason you get up. You want to be performing your genius to benefit the world and because if you don't you will get sick, grumpy and turn into a disagreeable person. We are all conduits of creativity, which is the divine.

Spirituality has a nasty little catch to it. Delusion can be huge. Remember we have to have equal amounts of light and dark to move forward and evolve. Where there is light there's an equal amount of dark and so often people avoid the shadow. They push it away, pretend to be something they are not and it comes through in manipulative, delusional ways. You have to do the work until the day you die, unless you are a great being. We need to constantly check into the truth and listen to others' feedback and our own intuition. That's one of the beauties of being a monk in the world. The world is constantly reflecting back to us the truth. This is our state where we need to adjust something. Secrets aren't ever a great idea.

The calling is an offering. It is not benefit driven, even though it's laden with every benefit imaginable. Abundance, the true meaning of abundance, comes when you live your purpose and are so in love with what you're doing that all your needs are taken care of.

### I'm scared because I love and want to do everything.

Oh my goodness, I totally understand this one. FOMO, or Fear Of Missing Out. Take the time to work out your genius, talents and passions and put them together into one service to start with. Then work from there. Otherwise you're going to end up too scattered and nothing is going to get off the ground. If you meditate on it, you will see the links leading to something specific. It is a difficult discipline when you're multi-creative. I'm one of those and being terribly creative isn't always helpful. You need to hold overall one thing and let everything else be branches extending from it. Trust that you will experience everything in the journey and all will be taken care of and you'll be given more than you could imagine.

I love that about the universe. Our minds aren't capable of knowing what we could have. That's why we surrender and let the universe deliver because it's always better.

### Actions to take:

Look at your daydreams and night dreams as a child or an adult. Were they trying to tell you something? What did you dream of doing most? Even if it caused you fear, like in my work, my story. What is stopping you from doing it? Fear? Then get help with the fear and have a look at self-worth issues.

Ask your friends what they love about you. Get feedback. It's a fantastic thing to do. Sometimes we're not aware of how we portray ourselves to the world. It could be that they say to you, you light up a room, or it could be with my friend that you're brilliant at finances. It could be that you're confident or that you make people feel a certain way. See how you can bring these skills into the world for all the benefit. We usually take these the most for granted and don't see the value and worth. We focus instead of something tangible, like 'I have a degree in medicine and can work as a doctor', which can leave you utterly miserable, tired, fatigued and grumpy. Yet your real skill was in something else. It was that you were funny, you made people laugh and maybe you should be looking down that road instead.

Dedicate every day, every minute, to your purpose, no matter what it is. Let it pull and inspire you. It is your reason for waking up in the morning. Write down what that is and reread it every day. Remember this is about taking our heart and soul to the world as us. Be graceful, grateful and never give up, unless God tells you to. And please, never force yourself to fit into a particular shape for somebody else. This is particularly important for women, as we often think we need the security. We're in a new era, whereas that is old-world thinking. Women, we don't have to do that anymore. We don't have to be afraid and should no longer hide behind a man and put all that pressure on him to have to look after us. If we want equality, we essentially need to follow our purpose.

If your purpose is to be a stay-at-home mother, fantastic. That's all that matters. If your purpose is to be a corporate person, awesome. Women are now being called to be independent. We no longer disempower ourselves and put our life in the hands of another person. For some, this is a stressful transition in society.

We need to be She-Monks and thrive. We need a certain discipline, routine and practice. We need to be stable and grounded. We are committed to presence. Presence takes care of everything. No matter what is happening in our world, it is only temporary. We bring the eternalness to it. Stillness, grace, passion, purpose. Our home life is very important. How we manage it is part of the work.

Journal the questions I mentioned above and spend time reflecting on them. Brainstorm and workshop them.

Be okay with the fact it may not be your time yet. That can happen. There's more life experience to have. For your unique genius and gift you may be in the right place at the right time, gaining important information. There are no time limits and there is no pressure here. Take time out of the equation. Go instead with what's coming up. Whatever you do, watch out for pushing and forcing. That's an indicator to stop and be present.

## Chapter Six

# SPIRIT TOOLS

Mystical tools help the healing process. They're simple and often what we take most for granted. We've all come into this world with things we need to heal and most likely have had life experiences that require our full mystical and spiritual toolkit. Living in the world, we need these more than ever. Healing and growing with grace has a wonderful purpose: we create love and peace at home and within ourselves. Embrace the time-honoured universal spiritual tools.

These are the foundations of being a She-Monk and of healing and living with consciousness. They are the day-to-day activities we need to do to clean up our energy and stay anchored in the Self. Interfacing with the world we sometimes swallow the feeling and the impact of everything around us. We are often empathic and sensitive and we feel the suffering of others. We take on the suffering of the world. Can you relate to this? Do you know what it's like to be inexplicably sad or flat after taking the world on your shoulders? We become unconsciously hooked in and start to lose energy. Eventually we go down. However, when we use these tools, we create a lightness of being and return to wholeness.

Using some foundational spiritual tools means we can potentially live longer, healthier lives. We clean up negative energy and take out the hooks. We have a desire for mastery in this world and a mindful approach to the forgotten arts of living is the training. The greatest spiritual tool of all time is forgiveness. How often have you heard that? How often do you do it? When we interact a lot with others and live a full life we are often not aware of just how much we need to forgive on a regular basis. We don't forgive because we literally wait and save it for the big stuff, not noticing the small stuff that can snowball in the background. Even when we know forgiveness is the answer, we don't want to give up any power that we get from holding a grudge, from being right and justified. We don't want to admit that we didn't need to react as much as we did. We want that person who did something to us to pay and if we forgive them, we feel like we're telling them that they've done something right. Can you relate?

Forgiveness done properly is a learned skill and is initially hard. It can be easy in superficial ways, but deep down many of us want to hold on. We want to hold on because we want that person to feel the sting. We want that person to feel what it's like to have love disconnected from us. Unhealed issues that require forgiveness can change the direction of our lives and keep us in a loop of suffering. They go down to a cellular level in the body and can cause disease.

Mystical tools are about living in and healing the heart and being present to our minds, our actions and the world around us. Often our actions and desires have come from the mind and we've completely lost connection with our earth, our cycles and our routines. I believe we don't even know how to nourish ourselves any more and we have paid a price.

> 'Be soft. Do not let the world make you hard. Do not let pain make you hate. Do not let the bitterness steal your sweetness.'
> **– Iain S. Thomas**

If we could all do this then we have a shot at world peace. I ask what it would take for people to live by this and use it as a reference, yet I find even with clients that it takes a fair amount of inner investigation to find exactly how much is going on, tucked away inside. They become certain their issues are a particular something so we delve into their inner world where the real issues are festering away.

Here you see another angle to using the manifesto. Often we ask ourselves, in this moment before the lower mind takes over and messes things up, 'What the hell do I do to be the best possible me?' In the example of love, the manifesto says, 'I will be love.' So how do I love? How do I keep my heart open? I need to let go of this. I need to forgive.

Well, when we can't find solutions like forgiveness, we end up carrying that situation like a ball and chain for the rest of our lives. We start using it as a reason to be small and we start sharing our traumas and outdated hurts with other people. Self-righteousness or revenge or anything like that is only fleeting. They don't cause happiness. They are simply power trips in the moment. Bummer, hey?

Anger, resentment and withholding love makes you sick. The more spiritual work you do, the bigger the price. I find spirit knows to expect more of you and the consequences are higher. Blame can feel like it makes perfect sense, as can self-righteousness. They can be difficult to catch but once taking on a commitment to spiritual practice and using spiritual tools we become present and better at catching them and bringing in awareness. Otherwise, we are basically wasting our lives, our opportunity to grow, evolve and expand. To go home. Holding on, reacting and not wanting to set yourself and others free is to be close-hearted and unspiritual. It's not the way of the She-Monk.

Healing tools are anything that helps take us back to the Self, to home, to love. We all have different varieties, depending on the different spiritual practices that we have done, but this is the basic definition. I find these tools are the same no matter where you come from. They are the things that give us a higher perspective. A She-Monk does these practices routinely. That is part of our commitment. We look at what I call the three centres of creation or manifestation. We go to the heart, the mind and the gut with an intention to return what we discover back to wholeness. Wholeness is, in fact, wellbeing and happiness. Happiness is wellbeing.

No matter what state we are currently in, wholeness holds the key. We can heal much of the energy and imbalances by focusing on some of the key tools. The mother of all is forgiveness. There is a cracker of a saying: 'Holding onto anger is like drinking poison and expecting the other person to die.' My teacher had another great saying: 'When we point the finger at another there are three fingers pointing back at us.'

Hold up your hand and point at the wall the way you would point at another if arguing or blaming. Can you see and feel the negative energy running straight back into you? Great to remember and catch.

What tools do you already have to make you present, to open your heart and to bring you back to wholeness? Mine predominately include meditation and prayer. I have different varieties for different functions. I have an altar and do a little ceremony I learned in India called a puja when I need to let go of particular energies and imbibe others. I do breath work, or pranayama. I do self-enquiry, which is possibly the most effective tool I have and the best healing tool when I see people. I forgive. I send love and blessings, even silently, to God. I like to surrender and hand things over, to get God to intervene and take care of things. I take a day off. I spend time in nature. I do certain wisdom practices like hathapaka and alamgrasa, where I literally eat, swallow and digest the energies around me and transform them to love. Acceptance is a really big one. Out of all of these, I suggest checking in with your physical and energetic body, especially the heart. Forgiving yourself and those around you daily is one of the greatest practices we can do.

Stress and anxiety are in epidemic proportions. The majority of people are stressed out of their brains. I've been one and didn't know it because it's so the norm these days. How many of us are angry and unfulfilled and chasing things that we don't even care about or want? How many are caught in limited thinking, like zombies, because we don't want to dare to be different, to be the rebel, to be whatever it takes, to beat our own drum and be happy? How many of us get to middle age and get an overwhelming experience of this?

We hold bucket loads of overwhelming built-up dramas, meanings, emotions, obligations, traumas and memories and we simply can't, won't or don't know how to sit with them. Instead we force ourselves to take it all on. I like it when people who come to see me show their anger because it's pretty damn obvious they need help and they can witness that. Sometimes it's their last resort so they completely combust. The hardest ones are those who are really asleep. They're in complete denial and don't want you to see that they haven't got their shit together. They don't realise there's hardly any life pumping through their veins. They're in a holding pattern that is blocking joy. They come to me for something they think is a little offbeat, woo-woo, kooky and maybe fun. They think I may read a card for them or put crystals on their heads. Boy, do they get a surprise when I do none of that! The first place I take them is straight to their inner world to let them experience how they are feeling.

One of the things I notice working with women and many female groups is just how angry they are. They're unaware of just how much anger they have. We have anger for many reasons. One reason is that we're in this change of roles and new era of the feminine. We don't quite know what we're doing. We're very much still in transition. We're chasing, investigating and claiming empowerment. We're getting a little unbalanced with the load we carry and the amount of hats we wear and are more often masculine in the process. We are still stuck playing roles we are tired of.

We also have a memory of our history. I believe this is a big part of why women are so exhausted. These feelings come through like a memory. Just by choosing to be female in this life we inherit the traumas of what it has meant to be female throughout history. It's all part of the ongoing healing process. We are healing for generations. When I see how much women hold on to, and how they have no tools or safe outlets anymore, it doesn't surprise me they become caught in anger. I'd love to see less fight and push and more focus on healing the DNA and healing our hearts. Forgiveness is so important.

Another important thing is we need to find ways to not let the suffering of others enter our being. This is difficult as most of us are terribly empathic or empathetic. Compassion is a tool. Compassion is a very good use of empathy because it creates a detachment. We still care but it stops us from getting hooked in. We can witness, understand and have compassion for what must be a very difficult situation for the people struggling.

Compassion helps us see things from different perspectives and holds the space of acceptance and hope for them. Compassion is a way of staying present and being around big feelings. It even works when someone is having a go at you, when you see that there's trauma or difficulty, or when someone is trying to open up or a child is crying. You acknowledge them and meet them on their level. There is no judgement and nothing is perceived as wrong. That brings tremendous relief. You simply acknowledge that what they are going through is awful. You can't imagine how it feels. "Sweetheart, you must be worried" is much better than "Just get off it. I can't handle this right now".

Always try to find compassion for the situation you or others are in. Have compassion for the other people involved. Imagine how they feel, why they got so upset. When a person is angry it is because they are deeply frustrated; they are at their wit's end. They don't know how to handle what's going on. Their anger is a sign of disempowerment and it's a cover for fear. Compassion creates spaciousness. It helps us relax and see emotional hooks, those little snags, those webs we've been caught in that, if left unattended, can run rampant in our heads, keeping us in the drama.

When I was first going down the road of getting to know myself I discovered that during my nightly showers my mind would wander to things that happened ten or twenty years ago. I didn't like these and would obsess over them while not being present. I had no idea that my evening routine was causing me to drift off into unhealed areas. This usually led me into a cycle of emotions and stress and made it difficult to sleep. It was extraordinary to witness.

When I got present to it I was able to stop it, bring awareness and diffuse the emotional reactions. The best way to do this was to tell myself that what I was doing was unproductive and then to forgive that person and remind myself who I am. To let it go I would say, "I no longer want this" and then I saw myself breathing love and understanding into the feeling and vision. Sometimes if it was really strong – this had been a long habit, you see, and it didn't want to give in too easily – I'd literally envision myself cutting a cord between the present me and the drama I'd created or remembered from years ago.

Is there a time of day or an activity you have that causes your mind to go places it shouldn't? Daydreaming was always a skill of mine. Somewhere in my life's journey, daydreaming in the shower or bath at night turned into an unhealthy mental discipline where I processed negative emotions I wasn't aware of. This is another part of getting to know thyself. We need to catch ourselves when we go down or lose the right perspective. The more you do it, the more you'll free up that energy. My teacher once said we're born with a particular bank account of energy. You could call it karma. We take the energy out, but we rarely put the same energy back in. We can't afford to have things draining our energy. Usually these are attachments we've formed on a subconscious and energetic level. Seriously, catch it and you'll be surprised what you're wasting precious time and energy on. It could even be a person that we crossed in primary school that we're still holding onto. Have compassion and forgive yourself.

Another wonderful tool is to make an intention every day to ask for divine assistance. We're not alone. Why do everything alone? Even in the writing of this book, I woke up at four o'clock in the morning and experienced anxiety. I couldn't work out why I was stressed. I meditated, but was still stressed. How bizarre. My next step was to do some self-enquiry. I asked, "Okay, where is this feeling in the body?" My heart was screaming at me. I looked at the heart and asked "What's wrong? What do you want to tell me?"

And with that an image popped up of a great being on the other side, someone I connected to in India many years ago. I hadn't been paying much attention to him for some time, but to my absolute surprise he was in there saying, "We set this up. You're not on your own here. You have forgotten this is a team effort and that is why you are stressed. I'm here too." It plunged me into my heart and the stress literally rolled off my being. I even ended up having a little tear of gratitude and recognition. It was so beautiful. I saw the help was there waiting for me to pause and let it in.

So much relief can come from realising that we're not alone. There is always help available. All we have to do is ask and let it in. Another great reason to forgive and unhook is that it frees up energy. This is important because many people wrongly use the idea of karma.

People often get confused about karma and have the wrong idea about it. We do much of this work not only because it's dharmic, right living and healing but because it helps us with karma. Karma isn't about punishment, as people like to think. These people have turned it into something like sin and judgement. Karma simply means there's a cause and effect for the choices we make. If you make a bad choice, then you're going to have to make it up on some other stage on the energetic level. It is a brilliant, ingenious system to get us to eventually not want negative karma, to not keep ourselves wading through mud and to finally become responsible for our lives. It encourages us to create as little negative impact as possible. We can transcend and transform karma by using simple mystical tools like forgiveness, awareness, meditation, acceptance, compassion, appreciation, prayer, etc.

With karma, when you put the brakes on and heal blame, jealousy, resentment, anger and move to a clear space holding love in your heart, you rid yourself of that energy that was once draining and blocking you. It falls back onto the other person, the one who's still stuck. If that person is holding anger or resentment, then it's squarely put on their lap and their shoulder. In an abstract way, this is an act of love. Hopefully they will want to move past it and heal too.

If we're She-Monks who are going to do as we say and be what we want to be, we must remember to have the peace and equanimity of the monk. We need to be fully alive and engaged in the world, do whatever it takes to keep a clear heart space and then put that tool in your kit and share it with others.

Another great tool is learning how to hold the space with another. This starts with active listening. Have you ever shared a problem with someone and felt deeply heard, felt understood and not judged? That is one of the most beautiful experiences ever. It takes someone with a sense of who they are, someone who works to not get disturbed and perturbed about the emotion you are holding. They are listening with compassion and know who you really are behind the issue. Their centre isn't rocked and they know how to hold the space and listen.

This is something I found extraordinary about my teacher. Sometimes I would be going through a difficult time. Sadhana (spiritual practice with grace) is no joke. There's nothing easy about it. If someone says sadhana is easy, I think they're taking something. Occasionally I'd go in there really upset. I'd be like, "My partner has just done this" or "My son was injured". Sometimes I was even furious at my teacher and yet every time, to my surprise, he would sit and listen. He wouldn't throw anything back. He wouldn't get defensive. Even if I was verbally throwing things at him, he would sit and listen patiently and show compassion. And he'd always say, "My dear, that sounds terrible. No wonder you're frustrated."

As soon as he said this, and as soon as I realised someone had actually listened to me and acknowledged how I was feeling, I would be over it! It was amazing. I'd even burst out laughing. Or I'd exclaim, "Oh my god, what have I done?" and I would see who I was being. My teacher's great emotional mastery became the benchmark for me.

My son once went through a very difficult time. When he turned fourteen, he was sad about his parents' divorce and how his father had abandoned him on an emotional and supportive level. It became too much and he went through a difficult phase of severe anxiety and panic attacks. I had to watch this amazing, bright, talented and loving boy turn into this dark, angry, self-loathing person. It was very challenging. No one knew what to do and neither family was there to help. They were instead judgemental. They didn't know what to do. *I didn't know what to do!* I didn't know how to help him or what to say. How do you watch your child go through such turmoil, such intense struggle, especially as a single parent, and not be torn or take on the grief?

Hold the space. I realised I had to make him not wrong, not different or not weak or strong, none of it. He was very strong. All I could do while he was being angry, dark, bitter and uptight, or if he was having a panic attack, was to remember that he hasn't changed underneath all of that. He's still the same amazing, bright, talented boy. When I did this I saw very clearly that there was a way out of this for him. I held that space and listened. I spoke to that part of him that was hungry for wisdom, hope, love and joy. To me, what my son was going through was deeply karmic. It was a soul contract he made before coming here. With the right environment, he would get what he needed and learn. He did. He is incredible and, eighteen months later he was fine and now years later, not only has he never had another episode, but he's become determined to help others deal with similar issues.

Don't get me wrong. I was incredibly worried and blamed myself at the time. My whole role as a mother, though – as a spiritually connected She-Monk mother who deeply loved her child – was to hold that loving space *while I was around him*. I had to trust him with everything that I had, trust that he knew what he was doing, and help him know that I loved him even though at that time he was very difficult to love. It was a huge lesson. I stopped everything. I stopped controlling, stopped pushing and I treated him like a different person. There's nothing like parenthood. As our children grow, we have to adjust our ways of being at different stages around them. They're not always children. They become young adults and their needs change. I think kids are our greatest teachers!

If we're following love, self-love and whatever it takes to be self-loving, then the tools will reveal themselves. Self-love is even a relatively new topic. With the epidemic of stress and anxiety, the need for teaching and learning about self-love is at an all-time high. Self-love is a tool. It goes in my toolbox. Put it in yours right now. See, it's not some tricky esoteric tool. It's a *collection* of tools, like a Swiss army knife, and it is fundamentally important. I actually didn't know about self-care. No one ever taught me. In my family, it was frowned upon. Strange, my grandmother was a genius at it. I think she wrote the book. But my parents were complicated about it.

Learning to understand the need for self-love has been quite a learning curve. It's amazing how, as a devotional person, I found loving God and others so easy yet I had to learn how to accept myself and treat myself well. None of it was natural. I had to learn little things like getting my hair done, knowing that I deserved the right foods, sleeping in and having 'me time'. It got to that point where I had to schedule in me time; it was non-negotiable. A coach had to point that out to me! Can you imagine getting guidance in how to log into your phone and set an alarm for personal downtime? What happens to you at the thought of you time? Are you already onto it or, like me, do you need a little nudge? Please do it. Right now, book in some self-loving you time. Do you go on annual retreats? Do you like going swimming or kayaking? Whatever your activity is, meditation is the best tool. It deals with the mind and helps you live in the present moment.

Remember also to laugh and smile. These are tools and both need to be in your toolbox. I have a laughing list on YouTube – comedy lightens me up. Appreciation and gratitude are tools that you've no doubt heard a lot about. They can effectively rewire our neural pathways. Grab a journal and note at least three things every day that you appreciate or are grateful for. Every time you're in a difficult situation and know you can't move out of it for the time being, clear the energy and allow in some grace. This will help you find ways to appreciate where you are now. It allows you to grow and become an amazing person. Show gratitude to those who've shown you where you need to work on yourselves.

One amazing tool that I need to mention is seva, or service. Our purpose, growth and insights all point in the direction of being of a service in this life. Once you know God and are still in the body that is where all roads have taken you. What's left now is to be of service to humanity. Service and devotion mean that you can always try to find a way to help someone else that is worse off than you are. When down, look at who you can lighten up. This gets the focus off you and brings in spiritual energy, which works as much on you as the other person. Pretty neat.

The more intricate yogic practices I did for many years are what gave way to understanding the simplicity and mysteries of consciousness. Remember, I'd done a lot of work that paved the way for this new direction. We all have to do the practices and have them in a formula that works for us and our nature. Look for the best spiritual direction you can find and stick with it.

## I find I can be very judgemental even when I don't want to be.

When I see judgement coming up it means there is a bug in my heart to deal with, something to acknowledge or forgive. Sometimes it also arises because I'm painfully hard on myself. I throw that pain out as judgement to others. Some self-love will help because it softens the attacks on ourselves. See the real cause behind the judgement. I like to be very real about it. We can tend to deny that we judge because it's so not cool spiritually and yet I have met enlightened masters who judge. No kidding. Don't suppress something you observe. Simply sit with it and use it to guide you to what you really mean before blurting it out and blocking your heart. Judgement is the mind's way of categorising and sizing things up for us to compare. This can be lifesaving if we aren't yet good at reading energy. Generally, though, it means there's a germ in there. Let me give you an example. Once a week I go with my kids to the huge supermarket down the road. It's a major event, a guise for bonding.

When I pass people or get to the checkout, I'm already sizing people up and making assessments based on the contents of their trolley! The wellbeing coach in me is fascinated. I can't believe what people buy. It costs much more money here in Australia to eat well as opposed to eating poorly and people make horrendous decisions based on price, apathy, addiction and lack of knowledge. Judgement can be a habit. I love to look back in my trolley and feel good that I'm stretching myself to buy the best ingredients and keep processed food to a minimum. You will never see sweet fizzy drinks or frozen meals in my cart! I can get quite critical of such things in my mind.

What do I do? Confession: once upon a time I was a bit radical. That's not healthy. The tendency was strong so I had to turn it into something useful and not be a loony about it. I turned it to a blessing, a prayer. I send a prayer to the person who's ill and overweight, or underweight and twitching. I pray that they love themselves enough to buy better food.

I send them prayers and wishes of abundance to override their lack and I tell them in my mind how beautiful they are. Behind judgement is a blessing and a core value. I value nutrition and get shocked when others don't. Sometimes I also remember to give them a smile. People know when you're perving at what they're buying so I take it as an opportunity to send a loving smile. Once in a blue moon that person will comment on how healthy my shopping is and how envious they are because it shows I care and can cook. That gives me an in to share some wisdom and tips.

Have a think about times you are prone to judgement. We all do it. See how you can turn it into something loving and productive. In what ways can you use your value for good? I became a wellbeing coach and plant-based wholefood chef running successful workshops on spiritual eating, healing and wellbeing.

When we live our purpose we're so happy in the moment and full of inspired doing that we don't tend to focus on what others are doing or getting wrong. It no longer suits us. Remember, expectations are involved here too. Look at what we want and take complete responsibility for working through it. Judgement and expectation are intertwined. Take that expectation, see it as a want and move it to the A list. That works every time. It's such a great way to fill your heart with love and joy. I get happy simply suggesting it.

### I find it so hard to be present with a houseful of kids getting messy and ready for dinner. What tools can I use here?

I love this. This is where it's at! This is you, the She-Monk, in action, and this is everything. You're expressing what an alive home life is like. Here is the best place to do the work. My suggestion is stop where you are, even if it's at the kitchen bench, chopping. Stop for a minute and breathe. Listen to the breath, the room and the noises. Allow it all, the kids, the commotion. There's nothing to push away or resist. Find the peace within. After lots of practice you'll automatically hold it and others will respond. The calmer I am, the calmer my kids are. Put on soothing music, light some incense. You'll find that it will change the environment. I love Mozart. I studied music as a kid, so when I'm frazzled I put some classical music on. It's clever with some kind of creepy musical relaxing subliminal message going on. My kids recoil from it and go somewhere else. If they stay, they tend to calm down and I'm happy with the support of this magnificent music. Chanting music works the same. Start singing Hari Krishna at the top of your voice and soon see what happens to the room.

## What do I do if I'm overwhelmed with emotion and have to go to work?

Go back to the manifesto. Carry it with you. Have it on your phone, in your office. On there you listed the things that make you happy and feel good. See what you can do right now. Use scents, lights, music, even a joke. Nothing is better than the breath. If you can, lie on the floor for a moment. If you can't, simply pause for five minutes. Take stable, consistent, deep breaths while being aware of your body, the seat, the room, and see the energy calm your nervous system. Ask yourself what is the most important thing to do right now in that moment and do it. Trust it too. The universe will support it when we are focused on what we most want. We get overwhelmed with too many choices and things to do. See if you can delegate. Ask for God's help. See what needs to be taken care of and do it.

Something wonderful we can all do and add to our tool kit is the Ho'oponopono. This lovely healing process is Hawaiian and means 'to make right'. It's one of the best instant circuit breakers and fast tracks to the Self that I've come across. There's plenty on the internet about it so have a look. I have adapted it myself, added one extra step to keep it complete in my work. Here's how I do it: take a moment for yourself. Put one hand on your heart, the other on your naval area and close your eyes. Breathe. Envision yourself in the cosmos as the true eternal being that you are: magnanimous and all-loving. Imagine spiritual energy pouring through you and out of you. Think of the situation you are stressed about and all the related thoughts and beliefs making it worse. Share that light energy with that situation and now say:

> *"I love you.*
>
> *I'm sorry.*
>
> *Please forgive me.*
>
> *I forgive you.*
>
> *Thank you."*

Hold the feeling for a moment.

The final tool? Breath. Pranayama. With no breath the rest is useless, right? We are alive when we take our first breath and we die when we take our last. A great Indian saint said that breath is the rudder of life. If you can focus on and control your breath you will gain so much mastery over yourself, your emotions and how you interact with the world. You yogis will know all about this. Get to a good yoga or meditation class. Look now at how you are breathing and witness what is going on. Is it slow and deep or shallow and fast? Breath reveals a lot. I teach a lot of breath work in my Anxiety to Grace course.

I request that you make a toolkit. Look at all the techniques and skills you have been given or invented over the years. I know you have a lot in you, more than you think. We have heard about compassion, forgiveness, judgement, honesty, etc., forever. We just don't do them. Sure there are many fabulous things like chakra balancing and energy work, rebirthing and cards, but they are temporary unless we do the heavy lifting. You want a great life and to heal? Look no further than your thoughts, feelings and actions and how connected you are to spirit.

Journal away. Write a list and make a file on your computer. Do one of my workshops or come to my retreats if you would like a deeper immersion into the practices. Find a spiritual mentor. Join a prayer circle or meditation group and keep it simple. Everything in this book is a tool. They are the exact tools I used to become a She-Monk. After decades of esoteric practices, reading, experimenting and an enormous curiosity to try everything, at the end of the day the solution was really, really simple: we need to be alert and responsible for our moods, for the grace flowing through us and for what we throw out there on others.

## Chapter Seven

# BEYOND MYTHS

The ultimate outcome for a She-Monk is to embody the I AM. To me, the biggest thing holding any of us back are the ridiculous beliefs and myths surrounding spirituality and enlightenment. These are misconceptions about what an enlightened being is, what they do and how they behave. How we see enlightenment, how we hold it and our mind's beliefs about it, trick us into thinking that it is something that it isn't. This affects our journey to She-Monkhood.

There will be a long, unnecessarily confusing road ahead of us if we don't take the time to bust these myths. As with any other area of life, be it finances or relationships, everything is up for renewal in this era of consciousness. This is especially true of enlightenment and self-realisation. When we are stuck with these unhelpful myths, we create blocks that hold us back. You can only achieve what you can believe. If you believe you need to be a certain way, wear a particular uniform and that enlightenment is limited to certain outcomes, then you are, in effect, holding yourself back. Busting the myths helps us to get real about what is so. The good news is that there is a way to create hope.

Let me say straight up that the awakened yogi, the monk, the spiritual aspirant who has one focused dedication, let go of thought processes and beliefs, and is open to what comes without judgement or doubt will get there. Determination is everything. Determination and grace, shakti or spiritual energy. At no time did I stop and think, 'Oh, I'm not a certain height or a certain weight', or 'I look a certain way or speak a certain way', or 'I have a particular personality or live in the suburbs therefore this self-realisation stuff isn't for me'. No way do I allow myself to believe that. We don't need those things to be who we want to be. All thinking like that does is close us to truth. I once heard that the entire universe fits into the fingernail of Vishnu, one of the Hindu Gods. I found that helpful. If you imagine the enormity of the universe and then it fits like a grain of sand into other universes it cracks open our small minds to the bigger picture, making us aware of how we hold onto our reality. My teacher said to me that the masters taught what worked for them. That doesn't mean it is the only way. We still need to be on the lookout for what works for us and that takes a heck of a lot of awareness and excellent discrimination.

When we bust myths, we free our hearts, minds and spirit! We blow our brains open. Our minds really are the universe already. We have three minds, two of which – the judgement and fear mind – don't work for us and one that can take us where we need to go. When we move beyond the boxing, the categorising, the doubt and the fear, we experience a level of consciousness that is beyond description. The good news about myth-busting is you can have a good laugh. You can say, "Oh my god, I've been holding myself back because I believed this and that!"

Most myths were designed to prevent our mystical experiences. Think about it. The major traditions. Once man got hold of the pure initial brilliance of a prophet or avatar the pure teachings became a religion and no one else was allowed to have those experiences. The original being never said that! Look at the Catholic Church, for example. They hunted, tortured and burned their mystics at the stake, calling them witches and devils, etc. We have inherited these crazy old – and not always *that old* – notions of what God, spirituality and enlightenment are. These myths were created to keep us small, controlled and dumb.

Another issue is that we tend to hear only from one belief system. Please know that I'm not just pointing at religions here. I've heard crazy stuff in the *New Age*, in tribal communities, old pagan backgrounds and the atheist movement. We hurl a lot at religion and can't see we have been stuck in something else. Dare I say that science is certainly a new religion and claims its authority like the church used to. We tend to follow it just as blindly. It's important to expand and see what happens in other faiths and not get too crazy about the one you are in. We hear one truth from one religious background or tribal community, or whatever it is, and we hold that as universal. But we're not necessarily getting the whole truth.

All that matters is what is being called through you and trusting the guidance. I moved through many faiths and settled for the one that spoke the loudest to me. My soul told me it would give me everything I needed. This didn't mean that it was, in general, perfect. Any institution with people is going to have issues. I found that anyone who was getting the call to take their spirituality creatively to the world would be blocked and talked out of it. This would happen after a lot of genuine sadhana, not for all but for many. But you have to step up and help be a light worker on the planet. You don't need to be speaking or looking differently. The iccha has come because you have a job to do, a purpose. Please go for it. I'm talking about listening to the spirit moving through you. Find the support you need to step into the world with courage and faith. I'll help you.

Very few people really know what enlightenment is. There's a perception that someone is a fraud if they don't look like Ghandi. If they can't walk on water or levitate or appear in two places at once then they're a fraud. A big problem with spiritual myths is they cause us to become stuck striving and pushing to be something. They take us in the wrong direction, somewhere that is not a match fit for who we really are. In the end we lose hope and become tired and jaded.

Somewhere along the line, the rubbish started coming in. We don't realise the cosmic joke. You see, whatever we're looking at, the I AM or universal consciousness is already us. I find in spirituality there's a hell of a lot of looking good, looking bad, dumbing down and trying to be humble. We think it will make us into something, that we'll be fabulous, we'll be the truth, that we are the right ones. We also have this crazy belief that enlightenment will take all of our troubles away. Heck, enlightenment might even make us famous! We chase this fictitious dream, which is really disappointing. What we are avoiding is the here and now and what is, in fact, real.

There is a brilliant Zen proverb: 'Before enlightenment, chop wood, carry water. After enlightenment, chop wood, carry water.' This is the total truth, people. It's nothing glorious, but it's utterly fabulous.

Believing myths means we are simply misinformed. I do however, like to find the intention behind why things are created. Sometimes the original meaning, even if 'off' came from a desperation for a situation to be better. Somewhere along the line, we may have also gained something from creating them – a payoff, so to speak. Like we hold onto a power trip or a wounding that gets us attention. We haven't taken the time to work out what we really believe, what feels right or wrong for us. We as humans can't help this sheep thing of following beliefs without question. It's important to follow – as in, if someone has been there and conquered it, we should ask what did they do? I've done this with great results. Spiritual energy is alive in someone who's gone the whole way to the summit. The female saint Anandamayi Ma said it is possible and usual for some to get liberated in a particular area, but they are not fully self-realised; that is very rare. If you can find a fully self-realised individual then believe me you will feel it. Do what they did while you are figuring out what works for you. But have the awareness to hear when something isn't right.

Unfortunately, some teachers and teachings can be very limited. They haven't experienced the summit or they are liberated in one area but not as self-realised as they think they are. I've heard teachers like this shut down and invalidate what someone else has been through. This makes me cringe. It is naïveté. This person may be really evolved but their particular experience doesn't mean they know everything. I recently read a current spiritual teacher say there is absolutely no such thing as a transference of spiritual energy from a teacher to a student. How awful! A transference of grace, even from a photo or statue, can have the power to awaken the ready and right seeker. It's called Shaktipat. I've experienced it many times.

Remember: what we think, we become. If you want to be the I AM, then direct your focus on that. Forget the rest and, in every moment, ponder the I AM. Be on the lookout for thinking we do all this work to become some kind of physically perfect person and that it's going to happen over night; that we will realise the Self and we're going to become this perfect person and all our diseases and imperfections are going to go away. An enormous myth surrounding enlightenment is that we think we'll one day wake up with all the answers. One day we're Gandalf the Grey, then we become enlightened and wake up Gandalf the White – long beard, white robes, dripping in spirituality and knowing absolutely everything about everything.

How many of you think you will never have anything go wrong again if you awaken then enlighten? Here's the sadness of the myths, where all the crap comes in. Here's where spiritual teachers think they have to hide aspects of themselves because, heck, I'm still human and things can still go wrong. That proverb about chopping wood and carrying water is the most beautiful thing. Zen got it right.

Let's now go back to creation itself. I like to think of it as the artist's palette. If you look around you, everything that you see has been created by the full spectrum of colours. That is creation. Creation is the full spectrum. Before I talked about our shadow side. We have the shadow and it goes all the way in all the different shades from dark back to light. Life is a painting. It has all of the positive and the negative. When we embrace and use all the colours, it becomes the whole. It has to be. When you're creating you can't leave anything out. That's the beauty of it. It's that simple. Instead of colours let's use experiences. Creation has every possibility in it. It has all the dualities – pain to pleasure, sadness to joy. The universe, our world, is what it is. When there is a cyclone or a fire we take a caveman approach and assume we have done something wrong. Or we think there can't be a god because how could God let that happen? We put our human values on God because that's how we hear on a basic level. It's like the Wizard of Oz choosing who to punish and who to bless.

You can't always pick and choose what you'd rather experience or what colour you want the world to be, but you can accept the world and how it works. You can bring the light of awareness to whatever is going on and still find the Self in all situations. As humans we're hardwired to go only for what gives us pleasure and will move away from pain. And in moving towards pleasure, we move away from the importance of the full spectrum of the palette, hence we move away from wholeness. I'm not saying we must suffer or go out to feel pain; I'm saying we can integrate it back to oneness. Be with it, accept and see the divine play in what has happened.

We are the palette. We are all the colours. We are equal parts light and dark. And we are constantly evolving. Where there is light there is dark. Every person carries within them the potential for anything. We are the cosmos. We're made from the same atoms and the chemistry and everything to do with the universe. We also carry within us what we see outside of us. We contain the addict, the cheat, the criminal, the lover, the genius, the comedian, the worker and so forth.

To be fully us, we have to embrace the entire spectrum: the good, the bad, the ugly and the fabulous. In my tradition at the ashram the ultimate state was called sahaja samadhi. That is to be supremely free, to be you as you are, so that when you go into that liberated state you are all of your being and you are free. Nothing changes; you actually become more *you*.

What I love about that is they're trying to tell us not to go into these big, ecstatic experiences thinking that's where we'll stay. That's only the transcendence part. When you're grounded you go back to chopping wood and carrying water. There comes a time when the ecstatic energy has to be grounded out and we go back to being purely us. That's the sahaja samadi.

A big problem with myths is they tend to create an image in our mind of what a spiritual or enlightened person looks like. Because of this we don't realise that the person next door to us, the man driving the school bus, could be enlightened because we're waiting for them to appear like Christ in a doorway, with angels singing in the sunshine and lambs running around. I was taught that there are enlightened beings, as Christ, as Buddha, in the here and now on the planet. Not everyone has the dharma or destiny to change the world like those big boys. There will always be extraordinary beings on the planet, like many of the saints. Look at the saints in all traditions. There are saints in the past and in the present. I use the word 'saint' to mean great being, but please know I'm not limiting this to what the church would call a saint. I love them. Researching and reading about them is where I started to realise all the bullshit going on in spirituality. They are as different in approach, size, shape, nationality, personality and looks as the colours on the palette. In some traditions, what makes a great being isn't just proof that they can play some kind of spiritual trick. We have become conditioned to look out for tricks as proof of a bonafide great being.

Leave walking on water for the big league guys. There is a possibility we can all do it, but because we can't doesn't mean we can't know and merge with God. Is any of this making you feel any better? Are you hopeful? You, as you are now, are enough, my beautiful friend. You can ooze grace no matter who you are, no matter where you are or what you are. Grace is an inside job between you and God. It's all about connection.

It's essential we peel back everything we think we know and allow the universe to fill that space instead. We must energetically open our vessel to receive love and get our mind's beliefs out of the way. That's it, in a nutshell. It – the receiving of spiritual energy, intel or realisation – can happen gradually or it can happen spontaneously. It doesn't matter. There is no right or wrong; it's simply a profound opening up to the present moment. If you do enough grace work, or have had past good karmas or have done spiritual work in a past life, then it should be quick and easier in this life.

Truth itself is beyond comprehension. It's beyond language. It's better to experience it for yourself than stay in the dilemma of trying to work out from what somebody is trying to say. How can you put all of consciousness into words? How can you fully express what happens to you in that moment? When you finally open your vessel up grace will fill every inch of your body and you will start to see the world as a divine play of consciousness. Some are very good at expressing this. They can convey it just in their being, in their stillness. I adore this. I have a connection to that great saint who appeared in my heart one morning. In India they call these extraordinary and rare beings Avadhuts. His name is Bhagawan Nityananda and he comes from a tiny town in India. He's where I get a lot of my inspiration. We couldn't be any more different. Not just because of where we live. He was male, died in the Sixties and wore a loincloth – not by choice, but because the villagers asked him to.

He was so absorbed in the Self that he did not care about how he was perceived. He just radiated grace, shakti or spiritual energy. To be in his company, people could become enlightened. He didn't discriminate based on class. He would see anyone who sought his counsel, whether they were poor villagers, government statesmen or wealthy, famous, Bollywood actors. He was even known to sometimes smear himself in shit and curl into a corner somewhere when crowds of people came to be with him. That's classic Bhagawan. There is no filth – only what is in the mind. He is far from the norm of what we think a saint would be.

We never stop being human. Sorry, guys. I've heard enlightened teachers say they stopped being human, that they've transcended the ego. Again, for the rare ones maybe, but don't get lost in that. You can end up running around in circles. I don't believe you can fully do that until you die. We have doubts, our human tendencies and we still have our quirky personalities while we're here, so why not make the most of it? Why not let that be who you are and how you express yourself? We are human until we die. Death is the real liberation. Some say it's the real creative birth because we're going back to who we are.

> 'Liberation is always and only inside each person. It is that dynamic stillness in which there is no external identification, but only an all-pervasive awareness and pureness. There's no prerequisite for attaining perfection other than total commitment and one-point devotion to obtaining the highest state possible.'
> **– Swami Chetanananda**

There are so many crazy myths out there and the one that had a big impact on me was that spiritual people don't get sick. People are so hung up on that. I've heard and experienced this. I've even read it from so-called teachers who naively, arrogantly remarked that spiritual people don't get sick. I've been arrogant in the past about this. Look, the body plays out karma. I was gobsmacked when consciousness forced me to go to a deeper level to understand wellbeing. I've read about the lives of the significant teachers and great saints. Many of them were terribly sick. This gave me hope and, most importantly, helped me see that at the end of the day it's not about the body. Here's a mindbender for you: some of the beings, as an act of love, willingly took on the physical suffering of those around them. Before you scoff, sit and remain open. I once had a similar experience with a family member. We can't understand the full nature of grace. Trying to shove it into a box limits you. We are, in fact, beyond the body. That's where the truth lies. This body is temporary. We give it way too much importance. We can heal and prevent most things, but some things we simply have to go through. Death and illness are some of them.

The real power is in acceptance.

Another myth is what I call the golden Buddha myth. We think that if we're enlightened we're going to sit in peace and serenity like the golden Buddha up on a pedestal. We're going to shine and experience total equanimity in all moments. It's a statue! Think of the expectations that you're putting on yourself and think of what you're going to do to yourself when you don't pull that off.

Imagine having this wonderful moment of communion with God then you come back down to earth and think, 'Oh, hang on, why don't I look like the golden Buddha?' or 'Why don't I look like Christ with a little lamb in my hands?' 'Why am I not able to heal everybody who comes my way?' That's all crazy stuff, but deep down inside I think all of us have had a fleeting glimpse of this myth.

When we believe that we have to look like another or be like the big avatars we push away the big outcome for us. If I thought, in my naïveté and determination to work out who I am, that I'd be anything other than this manifestation of me at the end then I'd never have had the experiences of God that I've had. Don't deny yourself the beauty of grace or the chance to see how it manifests through you. You are the channel of spirit, pure and simple. That is it.

If you're doing the work and you're living in the moment, living with uncertainty and following the calling, you don't even have time to worry about how you look or how you should speak. If people start putting that expectation and judgement on you, then just send them love. It's their journey and their minds they have to live with. Have compassion.

Some people also mistakenly believe that if someone is psychic then they are also spiritual. Actually, being psychic doesn't make you spiritual; it just makes you psychic! Of course it's certainly a side effect of spiritual work. We call this a siddhi, a little spiritual gift that we can be given. There are many fun and heart-warming divination practices, but fixation on them can actually get in the way. Sometimes I love getting readings and predictions. I find it a lot of fun and, in the past, these have broken my worries and given me great insights. But I don't get distracted by it. The reality is it's a mystical journey. Grace is mysterious, and meditation and prayer are where it's at.

Another great myth – one that's similar to the golden Buddha one – is that people think you're going to end up as some kind of nice Christ figure. This simply isn't true. You're going to end up exactly who you are. Or possibly a more intense version. Your nature might transform in some way or it might not. What I have learnt from being around many realised beings is that being nice is simply a choice. Being nice is more about personal transformation. It's a hard one to hear, I know. We expect all enlightened and spiritual beings to be lovely and soft and warm always. It's not true and it is dangerous to think that a nice person does no wrong and is reliable. It's better to be real and be around people who are okay being who they are. You don't have to like it but, as with yourself, let them be them.

> 'Accordingly, man looks towards what is without, and sees not what is within. Rare is he who, longing for immortality, shuts his eyes to what is without and beholds the Self.'
> **– Vedanta Sermon on the Mount**

This beautiful quote is about keeping your eyes within, on yourself, your Self, your inner world. Welcome the grace and energy of another that has reached the summit but keep the mind and judgements out of it. You don't have to be them; you simply need to be you, all of you. It is an inside job, everything.

> 'It is not a dry attainment of mere power or intellectual knowledge. A love, which is illuminated by the intuitive wisdom of the spirit, will bless your life with ever-renewing fulfilment and never-ending sweetness.'
> **– Meher Baba**

What does this mean? The sweetness of the Self is like a little tap of divine happiness and joy. It is constantly running and is eternal. It becomes like a basso continuo. It's this never-ending hum, this beat, or spanda, this pulse of loveliness and you start to see the beauty of everything and everybody else and what happens to you.

How magnificent and lovely is this? What are we doing looking for gifts and qualities in others when it takes our eyes off what we most want? What happens to the body is about body karma. Spirit is beyond the body. How much weight do you put on the perfect body, look, size, colour, etc? Believe me, that's an illusion. Make God your number one A list want and go for it with everything you have. Nothing else matters. Let go of beliefs, thoughts, updates on progress, comparisons and outcomes. Use the teachings you have been given and start where you are.

## Surely life must get better.

Believe it or not, there is still a sadhana involved, a particular sadhana for enlightenment. We still have to go through this sadhana to ground us. A great saint in India called Rama Maharshi went to a cave for several years after his enlightenment experience. He didn't go through anything beforehand. He didn't go through any dark night of the soul, which is another myth you don't need. On social media you see particular groups of people saying, "I've had three dark nights of the soul and nothing has happened…" Once you've had one, you know you've had one. We may go through it in our practice or we may not. Or, here's something: we may go through it *afterwards* and it can take the time it takes. It might take several years, or even decades. Don't get so hung up on that. It's not a prerequisite. If we are stuck in what others dictate we close off what may happen to us. If we think that someone doesn't endure any difficulty after enlightenment, then we are missing the possibility of company with some amazing beings. We should not be too busy sticking our nose in the air, judging their very private experience.

I hear everyone these days has had some kind of dark night of the soul. No one really knows what it's like. Go beyond the mind. Ignorant people judge what they don't understand. It's all beyond the mind. I'm saying be open to how it plays out for you. Life will eventually get better. Not only in the way you see the divine play of everything and everyone. See them as shining beings of universal consciousness. You will go through great bouts of bliss or joy, but you still might have to go through some kind of sadhana.

**I feel that spirituality should be free. A real spiritual person, especially a monk, lives in poverty and chastity.**
Oh, fabulous. This is one of my favourites. How is that working for you? How is your abundance? How is it stopping you being that spiritual person, or the She-Monk? Are you going for gold? Are you staying away from that spiritual stuff because you don't want to touch poverty and chastity, or do you simply remain a consumer of it? That comes from the old monk world and it was needed at that time. We are living in a different era. It was delicate back then. In their evolution of consciousness, you would be drawn out by the five senses: by desire, by gold or by money. This was seen as evil because it would snap someone out of their deep contemplation of the divine, but this is not so anymore. We've come a long way. We don't need to be starving; we don't need to carry wooden bowls around our necks. That's all nice, but it's now part of a tradition.

Society also isn't as generous anymore. It's not so safe – particularly in the west. I live in a very lovely hometown where people are incredibly generous and they look out for everyone. It's a strong community, but if you went walking around with a loincloth on and a bowl, you'd be locked up and called crazy. We don't have it in our DNA like they do in countries like Asia or India. If they see someone who's having big spiritual movements, they will take care of them, nurturing the spirituality in that person and acknowledging that they are a potential great being. But this is not so in the west. We're so used to judging people and burning people at the stake. It's in our history. We don't like gurus. We nail them to crosses and we'll do anything we can to prove they're wrong. It's really, really sad.

If someone shows some piety and sincere spiritual achievement in India it's a boon, but in the west we label them as mad. We need to let go of these traditions. They don't serve us. I really doubt that they served back then. Be free, sahaja samadhi, as you are. What if money comes your way? Will you let it go simply because you believe you must live in poverty? *You must never suffer in the name of spirituality.* That is lunacy. That is dogma. That drives me crazy. If you are meant to be a business tycoon then fulfil that purpose. If you are meant to run a bookstore café, fulfil that purpose. If you are here to feed the poor, do that.

If money is your motivation then I question how spiritual that is. If power and domination, control and influence, is your motivation … again, is that spiritual? It may be religious, but not spiritual. What is the meaning you give money? Can money simply be an energy exchange? Can money be allowed to be what it is without the heavy emotions attached to it? In the Vedas they say that, in this era, money and gold is where maya or delusion reside. I say clean up your thoughts about money. Let it be and allow it in to help you do what you need to do. Too much money isn't necessary, but how can having enough to live well be a problem?

I believe in keeping things clean. I like to let go of potential hooks and money can be a hook. I have a great service and tonnes of experience. I like being a teacher and mentor but I have no desire to be anything else that requires being in a position of influence and power. I like the unfoggy clear boundaries of 'Here is a service. This is what it costs'. No giving up your life, your home and putting our lives in others' hands. I do my job. You do yours. Let's create world peace together in our unique ways.

Back to society and generosity. Church is free so we want all spiritual services for free. Be honest here: we get annoyed when we have to pay for a retreat or a workshop. I saw this so many times at the ashram. There were heaps of free events and services, but the really specialised events cost money – sometimes a lot. The ashram didn't get government funding like some big religions, so it needed these donations for survival. I was always amazed at how people whinged and complained that it should all be free. It showed more about the person complaining then it did the centre. We have screwy values when it comes to spiritual enterprises. If a religious group runs a one-week meditation retreat for a rock-bottom price, then that suits us. We don't realise they can only do that because they have given their lives up for it. They depend on tithing and donation and, in some extreme cases, people offer up their homes and possessions to help the causes. This can be wrought with issues, which I've seen firsthand. Keep it clean, guys! If it is someone's life calling to offer spiritual retreats, they have a genius, but they also have a home and mortgage, a partner and children. Why on earth should they give up on what is being called through them – the ability to charge what is right – because others want the poverty and the freebies?

I don't need to say too much more about it. Just look at the history and issues of embezzlement and sexual misconduct with priests and monks of *all* faiths. I rest my case. I think a business model is such an intelligent way to go about it. If we paid for services, then all that underhanded financial mess that has tainted so many groups goes away. Be upfront, be transparent, be humble and be okay earning your keep teaching people to pray or meditate. If you can't pay look at what is inside of you!

## If it doesn't make you magical and superhuman, then what's the point?

That's the ego talking. It's about freedom, breaking of samsara, the cycle of birth and death. Going home and staying there is now guaranteed. There's no more of this human stuff unless you want to come back. You can become free even while in the body, through the body, but some karmas of this lifetime will still play out. The way to transcend them is to not get hooked into them, to always return to love. Love is the gift. Love is the greatest siddhi or gift. Love triumphs. That's why I promote working out what you want, which is always an attribute of love, and then making a contract with yourself to be in any and all situations. Say, "Well, if I need to do this to pull it off, then that's where the spiritual practice is."

I know there are many myths out there. These are just the few that had an impact on me. Have a look. What do you believe? What do you judge about enlightenment? What do you think that person should look, behave and feel like? Go through each one of these and see where you've inherited it or created it. These are just like disempowering money beliefs, but you can clean them up with awareness and release them, set them free. You'll be setting you and everybody else around you free. Just like with enlightenment we need the spaciousness to be us, as us and to create that for others. The best place to start is with the crazy myths and beliefs we have around our spirituality. Believe me, if someone tries telling you what you should do, how you should look, keep walking. That isn't spirituality; that's dogma.

Start to see yourself as the best expression of you. Visualise it. What feeling and words describe it? Write them down and let them guide you. That's a much better focus. If you want to be good, start being honest. Take the steps in this book. Choose to be good. Choice is what creates karma. Recognise, accept and be real. It's very simple. Just do the work. Be the best you possible and see where that takes you. And in the process, remain a member of this world. Don't hide away. We want you. We need you. You are fascinating. If you're after magic, look for the miraculous. Go beyond the mind and look at the shift in your perspectives. Clear the heart, let God take over your being. That's a miracle. There are many paths to God. We all have our unique personalities that align with particular pathways to the divine. Most importantly: commit to it. Follow that want. Make that the middle of your mandala.

You want freedom, enlightenment and constant communion? Then that is what you must go for. That becomes your manifesto. Stay part of the world but don't get lost in it. Be a She-Monk.

## Chapter Eight

# FOLLOWING GRACE

Whatever happened to good old-fashioned grace, to spirit? In this era we're talking a little more clinically. We are missing the awe and wonder of good, old-fashioned God, stuff like grace. Grace is an energy, a force, and it is way beyond science. It's beyond rules.

It's not clinical. Grace is rich, benevolent. It is the force of love that acts for us and with us. It is alive. It is our partner and our lover. I use grace as a more universal word for Shakti or consciousness. They are one and the same but I found people didn't understand when I spoke about Shakti. They certainly understand if I use the world Grace, though, and it has become one of my favourite words.

Grace is always looking out for us and our best interests. It is so mysterious and that's why I love it. It is definitely a mystical, alchemical energy. It is active. Following grace is important because it keeps us in sync with the pulse of the universe, or the spanda, to use the Sanskrit term. Spanda is my very favourite word. It is ancient and basically means vibration or energy. The yogis call it the divine pulse of the universe. There is nothing new with these modern energy and vibration teachings. Only the language changes.

Once you taste grace, see how it works, see that we're never alone and see how alive it makes us. We will start to do whatever it takes to get more of it. When we live in a surrendered state, grace does so much better for us than we can do on our own. When I say surrendered, I'm not saying you should do what someone tells you to do that doesn't feel right.

I'm not telling you to become a victim or a martyr. I'm saying to take away resistance, go beyond beliefs and thoughts, and follow your heart. Grace is very humbling and experiencing a power greater than ourselves is its gift. It blows away the cobwebs of our being and all the limitations. We know what we can have and who we can be.

The beautiful thing with grace is that we start to see that the universe is receptive. It gives and it receives. Love is active. There is reciprocity to life that is focused on grace. Grace is simply the beginning. It is the cause. It is creation. It is the middle and it is the end. Everything is manifest and is done so due to grace. There is nothing that is not Grace.

The only issue is our ability to see or experience it. We often believe that if something is good or positive, if it has a good vibration and energy, then it is Grace. If something is bad or negative it is taken down to a lower vibration. This means there is no grace, but there's more to the story. It means there has been a concealment of Grace.

Grace is the exact same word as love, remember, and consciousness. Consciousness is the stuff of the universe, the stuff that gets scientists stumped because they don't want to acknowledge it. But when they finally get there, which they will, when they finally acknowledge that which can't be measured we will have unity between science and faith. Won't it be gorgeous when science has its version of the genesis in a language that scientists can tolerate?

Remember what I said before: in the full spectrum of creation, both good and bad, come from Grace. That limitation, which they call Maya in yoga, is in the mind. It is our perception, our way of using the right mind that determines whether we experience grace or not and whether we see the world as a magnificent manifestation of it.

> 'We cannot get grace by virtue or so-called merit. The worst sinners have received grace and become pure and glorious. Purity is not a precondition for grace. It is the flow of grace that makes the heart pure. When grace comes, it comes. Not because we deserve it, nor as a reward for practice, but only out of God's boundless mercy and love.'
>
> **– Swami Ramdas**

How magnificent is that?

> 'Grace is pouring on all alike. Some receive it and some do not. Some people open the windows of their hearts to receive grace and benefit by it, while others keep them closed and so they do not get it. But even to keep the windows of the heart open, we require inner aspiration and longing, which can come to us only through his grace.'
>
> **– Swami Ramdas**

Without recognition and appreciation of grace, there is no real mastery or mysticism in life. We've been caught in a loop, in the dryness and success of the world. Not being aware of grace indicates that we're disconnected, asleep. Maybe we have a closed heart or we've been hurt. Our minds have switched to a limited mind. The thing is when we forget grace we lose the wonder and awe of a child in the world. Do you remember being like that? Do you remember seeing fairies in the garden and believing in Father Christmas? A child understands that there is power beyond us. They don't question it.

We forget that there is a power beyond us and become very limited.

Grace heals. A great healer simply channels grace and can create the space for someone else to channel their own. Grace helps us appreciate and have joy in the world. It makes us grateful to the universe.

Spirituality is not really that complex. I've got a cup analogy. I use this analogy in every class I run and with every patient or client I have. I show a picture or hold up a cup. The idea is that once we are awakened, once we have the calling, we fill that cup with love, which is grace. That is the whole spiritual practice: to nurture the cup. If the cup becomes cracked, grace will leak out and then we have to find ways to patch it up and reseal it and refill it with more grace. It's better to become masterful of your own life and seal that cup. Then we can clean up with the tools I was talking about before. Look at judgement and forgiveness, and unhook the emotions, dramas and energetic pulls of our world. Spend time in meditation and communication. Those things fill our cup with grace. Love unconditionally as much as you can.

The cup is the mind and the liquid – let's say it's coffee – is grace. When the cracks appear, they've actually appeared in the mind. For those with a sensibility to the mystical, grace can occur naturally. The idea that God is a guy who hands down judgement and punishment and thinks of us as sinners is a myth. I couldn't think of anything more horrific. Thank goodness people are free to choose to leave those sorts of teachings. To me there's no grace in that. There's nothing universal. They are not the words of God. They have been misconstrued somewhere along the line and turned into tools and weapons. Spirituality like this is the very worst weapon!

Any kind of line like that comes from the mind of a man. The universe is so benevolent and kind and is terribly impersonal. It just does what it does. Why should we be any different to the rest of the creatures living on this planet? What makes us special is our minds and the ability to transcend past it to our pure mind and to pure nature. We must not think that God is separate to us and that we're special because we are the only smart ones who follow Him. Believing that we will never suffer again if we are in complete service to Him is very small thinking. It comes from fear and not presence, awareness.

Let's just dig a little deeper into grace. I really need to let you know something. Grace does not see colour, class, education or age. It couldn't care about your upbringing and doesn't know anything about your financial situation. It actually does not discriminate ever. It is constantly pouring its love over each and every one of us. A convicted criminal in jail has just as much access to grace if they are perceptive and aware as someone sitting in church. With grace there is no one religion, no one way; there are no sets of rules. I don't care what background you're from. If you start thinking that you have the one right line of thinking or the one right path then delusion has set in.

Grace is beyond all restrictions and rules. There are some basic foundational laws of consciousness but, in reality, the greatest way to look at grace is just with awe and wonder. And hope. Hope is a wonderful place to find yourself in. It's like a pause or cadence point in music. Suddenly anything can happen. If you've been disconnected and suffering, find the hope, as that's what invites grace. When we find hope we can start taking the sunglasses off to see the light.

Grace is all things manifested. It is pure creativity. It is nurturing. It is love. Can you see that it is all the aspects of God that represent the divine feminine? Hence why some people say that it is the divine mother. God isn't, in fact, a man. God is masculine and feminine, but there are two distinct energies. There's the dynamic stillness, which is considered the masculine side of God, and creation, which is everything that springs from that. This is the feminine aspect.

In my tradition this was also called Shakti. Everything that we see around us is the divine mother, the goddess of creation. Everything that the five senses can detect is actually a play of consciousness, but the practice involves looking beyond the five senses. This is why we are She-Monks. We use the world to show us where we need to do the work, but we are still aware of the need for inner time, contemplation, and rest; for detoxing from the world. It's important to spend time in meditation, in nature, in contemplation and in prayer.

Shakti and grace are exactly the same as consciousness here. Consciousness is absolutely everything. Whether it is the stillness of the masculine or the activity of the feminine. Everything is consciousness. She is the muse of my mandala. When I opened that book and saw the mandala of consciousness I simply saw four concentric circles. In that everything made sense. Consciousness, or grace, is form and formless. This whole dual thing, if you know what I mean. Are we one with God or is God a separate entity? People become so caught up with it, though it never really fazed me much in practice. I didn't really care; I simply accepted both of them as a play of consciousness. I would instead see where liberation was. If it was possible for someone to see God as outside of them and it was possible for someone to see God through their higher self or within them and realise the Self, then both must be right, so what's the fuss? This is what I love about the tradition I come from. The best thing to say is "It's a play of consciousness. It doesn't matter."

Leave everyone to whatever floats their own boat as long as it does no harm to others. There is no right or wrong, but I do have to say that in my relationship with the cosmos, my experience of grace, of God, it was beyond form.

This was helped greatly by something my teacher said at some stage in my sadhana. I remember sitting there one night with what was called a Satsang program. I had been contemplating the form and the formless and he said, "Look at the Shiva lingam." This egg-shaped stone from India is meant to represent the formless aspect of God, or Shiva. He then said, "Behind all form is the formless. Behind all manifestation is consciousness." This completely blew my mind and I suddenly saw the space. I saw the delicate space, the infinite space between all things – from atoms to black matter to the space between my breaths and words. That divine moment, that eternity, is in the formless. For me that's where the truth is. I went into some great, ecstatic state. That was joyous for me. I felt the expansiveness and oneness, and the complete intelligence of the universe.

I don't need to explain it, coming from astrophysics or quantum physics. I don't need to have it proven like that and I think that one day, they will come to it, Einstein had already done that. They'll see and have awe for the wonder of grace here. That's why I enjoy helping people so much, because I get them in touch with grace. They come to meditate with me, to have a session and they leave having had an experience of grace.

Moving from the form to the formless is a very powerful way to access grace because grace is matter and behind all matter. Another classic way is to consider the perceived and perceiver. What is being perceived is consciousness and who is doing the perceiving? Consciousness. This might bend your mind, but it lets grace in and tells the true story. The moral? Always go back to the witness, that which is silent and still and watching us. Go beyond the body and the senses. That is where we access grace. It is in stillness. And remember that grace is mysterious. We like to squeeze it into rules and boxes and categories, but it can't be boxed.

Grace is the realm of the mystic. Sometimes when it's our turn to heal at the most incredible soul level, then grace will turn our worlds upside down, as it did for me. A healing crisis can actually mark the beginning of the making of a mystic. Do not judge. Sometimes people go through hell and there is just no explanation for it. They may be lovely people who do all the work, have big hearts, eat well and move and yet look at this crap they're going through. I went through a period when people used to move away from me because I was always going through such deeply horrible stuff. In hindsight I can see the play of consciousness. I had chosen in this lifetime to move through a mighty load of karma and I did have some serious questions and a chat with God. I tell you, it wasn't always pleasant.

There was a time in my healing crisis, though, when I came across grace in another way. This is why I've become so much more universal. I came from a yoga tradition and when I had the healing crisis I ended up very much alone. I had no support, even though I had a partner and a community. I ended up being bedridden for months and months. At this time I was trying to work out if I was a failure. I asked, "Why did this stuff all happen? What is going on here?" I remember what started as me going to bed at night, always at a particular time. I'd close my eyes and contemplate just before going to sleep, as I've always done. But instead of sleep I started seeing these enormous lights. I've seen lights many times in meditation but these were different. Sometimes they'd flicker around the sides of my eye and sometimes they'd come up in front. Some were so bright, even though my eyes were closed, that I would have to squint really, really hard! Sometimes I couldn't handle it. I'd roll onto my side and this energy would move from my eyes to my ear. It would be like choral music in my ear. Then I'd roll onto my other side and I would hear another little noise. This went on for weeks and I started to enjoy it. I took little notice of it because I was too stuck in my story, stuck in the grief of being disabled and being incredibly unwell and feeling so remarkably unloved and unsupported. But the sound and the flashing went on. They started getting brighter and bigger and louder. Eventually the noise became a screeching. Then it was no longer pleasant.

One night, it didn't stop after a while, like it usually would. It was the middle of the night. I sat up and decided to talk to it. I said, "Are you a being? Are you trying to communicate to me?" As soon as I said that, it was like: 'Oh, hello. Finally! Thank God, she listened.' I saw these blobs of light, each one a different colour. They looked like the shapes of babushka dolls and they introduced themselves one by one. I kid you not! They said that they were deities, angels. I had never even thought about angels. They weren't even a part of the tradition I was in and yet here they were. They weren't white with wings, like the visitations I'd had in meditations years ago.

I call them my blobs (because it makes me laugh and that's what they were!), my posse of divine light, divine helpers. They are pure grace. I knew then that I was going through something very mystical, something outside of the normal context. I knew I needed to go through it, and that they were there to help me every step of the way, and they completely changed my healing journey. I totally surrendered to it, even though it was getting worse there for a while. Then these beings turned into green light. They turned into ants crawling all through my body and I knew, I just knew, that I was going to heal to the level I'm meant to. It's going to happen in the time it's going to take. All I need to do is make the most of the present.

With that awareness I was able to move towards my purpose. I stopped being hooked in by the story and the drama and the disease and the horror of the whole thing because I knew that grace was working with me. It was such a mysterious and fantastic thing, and so different to the other wondrous mystical things that have happened to me. It also took me completely outside anything I had known or experienced before. I saw that grace is bigger than any institution, than any person, any story.

I don't think we need to dictate whether grace is personal or impersonal. It's all grace, anyway. I like them both. It depends on my mood and what will bring me joy the easiest. Both are beautiful, so I do see merit in both dual and non-dual approaches. Sometimes I want to see God as something outside of me. Sometimes I have a chat to God. It might be God as man or the divine mother. My mother died many years ago, so it can be comforting to me to feel the hug of grace. It can be comforting to me to see God as someone I'm in a relationship with, that God is my ultimate partner and lover. I can also go into a bliss state and contemplate the stillness of the formless.

That's what I love about the philosophy of Kashmir Shaivism. It incorporates all of life. Life is very real. It's not an illusion. You don't have to see the world as an illusion. If it makes you feel better, go there. If it makes you feel sad that it's an illusion, don't go there. Just go wherever it is life-affirming. I'd rather you see everything as a divine play and accept the broad spectrum, the artist's palette of life, the light and the dark, the good and the bad, as the way our mind interprets everything. It's all the same sparkling consciousness and the same spanda is pulsating through all.

There are five life processes according to Kashmir Shaivism. We know that there's birth, preservation and destruction. There are actually two more. We have discussed concealment. So there's concealment and grace. For example, it is easier to see how, for most of us, consciousness is concealed. It is hidden from us as an experience of separation: that we are not one, that there is duality. A spiritual experience and spiritual attitude sees the grace, the oneness. Again we see that same sparkling consciousness in all. This means there is creation and that creation is sustained and preserved for a while and then it is destroyed, comes to an end. Everything comes to an end. Everything except consciousness itself is impermanent.

Destruction is still grace. The only thing stopping us from seeing that is that part of us that is ignorance, the concealment of grace. Concealment happens through the mind. We know it's present when there's fear, pain, separation, and negative tendencies running, or when we're contracted – as in pulled away – our love. If you find the idea of the first three aspects painful or stressful, then there is a concealment of grace. However, if you delight in the play of consciousness, then there is grace.

Keep your eye out for that. How do we do it? Stop thinking. Seriously, no-think is the best way! I would love to make and sell t-shirts that say *Please no-think*. Everything is in the eternal moment, is in presence, where we best communicate and experience grace. All the answers are there. I remember one day asking myself, 'What if that thought wasn't necessary? What if that the meaning I gave that situation actually meant nothing? What would happen? What if I wanted God so much that everything anyone ever told me was just a lie?' You know what? That really helped. To my delight, whatever was bugging me would drop and I'd be returned to truth. Even if there had been an emotional plugging in the suffering stops and we move towards peace and equanimity. It can be as simple as that, if we let it.

Following grace is also the path of least resistance. Not only do we allow grace in and see everything as a play of consciousness but we become aware of our reactions. That which expands us is truth, whereas that which contracts us is not in this moment. Self-inquiry is the best process for this. Simply close your eyes and ask your body what is happening, what it is trying to say, what you want, what you think. You will feel a reaction. Even if you feel fear you can still feel an opening, an expansion, so you know that even though you may be nervous about say public speaking you see that it is in your best interest to do it. If you feel a complete *no* then don't do it. Drop it and see where the expansion is, the clear space of good feeling as I was taught. This diligence, this discrimination, is marvellous. It's mastery. It may show things you don't wish to look at or accept. That is a deal between you and your ego. The important thing is that you are present and following the grace.

## I want to feel grace. I ask but nothing happens.

Be still. Profoundly still. Feel the energy of objects and beings around you. It's too difficult if you're in your mind and pushing for a result that you have in mind. Ask for it. If you do I guarantee messengers will be sent to you too. I remember telling my son this. He said there's no such thing as divine grace, divine assistance. Then one day we had to go to a funeral. His friend had died and he was desperately sad. He was finally open to receiving my help with this so I said, "Ask God. Say, 'I want to feel grace, happiness, and my friend again. I want to know that my friend is okay.'" When we got home there was the most magnificent owl waiting for us on the doorstep. It was actually on a pole, just beside the door. I said to my son, "Here's your messenger." He stopped, looked and started to commune in silence with the owl. The owl stayed for a good five minutes. We were in complete awe about this extraordinary gift. The owl eventually flew away and my son felt so much better.

Ask again. Sit in silence. Wonder and look out. It might be an owl. It might be a song on the radio. It might be the love you feel coming from another. It might be the joyful experience with your child. Just feel the world around you and listen to your inner world. Watch with stillness. See how creation is always happening and bubbling up from the surface, like bubbles in a lemonade bottle. Feel the love you have for your partner. For me, it's my pet rabbit. He is grace. I feel the grace in his company; he's like a mystical woodland creature. Feel the heat emanating from the sun on an early spring day as it kisses our skin.

## How do I follow grace?

Watch your thoughts and feelings. What is your daily experience like? Move towards that which lights you up and expands you, that which makes you experience being universal. How can you be humble and keep your heart open? Broaden your mind and open your heart. When hurtful things happen to us we react and put cracks in our cup. Remember the cup analogy. Seal the cracks, forgive and meditate.

## I struggle to go to no-thinking or even good feeling sometimes.

While we're learning or going through trauma, which is demanding for even the most illuminated, it's best to start with where you're at. Point your compass to home. Follow my mandala. The body is a great place to start. Practise self-love. Be present to the sensations in the body. Sing, dance, light a candle, do some yoga or go for a swim to expand your feeling. Most importantly do some kind of devotional practice and do an act of kindness for someone else. These will help occupy your mind from over-thinking. They will lift your energy and open you up. Once we're in a better place and mood, opportunities will come to us. Those with active minds will know that mindfulness practices really work. The best one I have found is mantra repetition or 'japa'.

No-thinking takes practice. When you're dealing with a traumatic experience it can be easy as trauma thumps us harshly into the present moment. But every time you can choose to do mindfulness, you will see the thoughts go through like clouds in the sky. Or you can be like me and say, "That's not real. That can't be so. It is just a thought. I choose not to believe it. I just want to hold peace in this present moment."

Ask yourself, "Am I benefiting from the thoughts I'm having? Are they true? Are they taking me home or far from home? Are they trying to stop my experience of pain, loss and suffering?" If so then we're in the ego. We're not in acceptance of the present moment.

Ask what would be so if you simply decided that these things weren't true. Become mindful for a while. Try to stop thinking. Use mantra, as mantra is the greatest way to stop thinking. Totally absorb yourself in the simplicity of being, walking, doing and watch the thoughts drift off. Most importantly, appreciate each moment. Even if you can't feel it, grace is present because it is the moment. It created it and it created your experience of it. There's nothing that isn't grace. That's the funny thing. It's wonderful. It's trippy at first, but it really helps us appreciate the magic of consciousness here and now. Now see if you can hold that feeling for the rest of the day. If you're in a situation that's causing you pain, just say to yourself, "Grace is concealed here. Grace is in here. Please show yourself to me. What do I need to know in this moment?"

## Chapter Nine

# INNER CREATOR

L iving creatively and seeing the divine play from our inner lives brings relief, healing and joy. Life at its very essence is creative. We are here to live creatively, to do the work with our inner creator.

> 'You must not let your life run in the ordinary way. Do something that nobody else has done, something that will dazzle the world. Show that God's creative principle works through you.'
>
> **– Paramahansa Yogananda**

Living creatively is how we make ourselves stretch and grow. It's how we celebrate life and follow the spanda principle, the pulse of the universe. Living creatively puts us in alignment with that divine will, iccha, and its inviting grace as our life partner, our side buddy, in our adventures in this world.

When we are living creatively, we become our most authentic self; we become unashamedly who we are. There's so much freedom and joy in that. This is about complete freedom of expression with grace and style and it comes from our higher Self. Our inner creator finds fun and solutions with what we need. Living life creatively from our inner Self is another way we heal.

I've found that by living like this we can express and experience the beauty of life, which is grace. Happiness is living creatively, to lose yourself in creativity. From my experience, creativity brings aliveness and joy. If you want harmony, get creative.

Creativity is the active creating part of consciousness called Shakti or, again, grace. Creativity is problem solving. When we're not living with our inner creator, we start to get boxed in by life. I'm sure many of us know what it's like to wake up one day and say, "Are you kidding me? Is this what life is really about? Is this all? I'm ripped off! This is crap!" I don't care whether you own a house, have a great job, travel the world living out of a suitcase or live in a monastery, there will come a point where, if you're not keeping that creative principle alive, you will start to go flat, start to die inside.

If we don't use our inner creator we won't find inspiration or solutions to our everyday problems. We end up running around in circles with the same attitude and perspective that got us into the problem in the first place. This is so boring. Deathly dull. The only times I've lost my creative spark are when I'm really, really sick, or stuck in a situation where someone else had a bigger, more dominating energy that I thought I was unable to move away from. Luckily they're the times I most drew into my higher Self. Life doesn't need to be beige.

I love how Billy Connelly, the world-famous comedian, says, "Be anything, but don't be beige." I'd fully have to agree with that. If you're not using your inner creativity, you're not using your full capability and capacity. You're not in flow. Creativity's a state of flow. There's no juju, whatever that means. It's a one-way ticket to becoming depressed and being prone to anger, sadness and anxiety.

Here's the thing: most people are unsatisfied and have been corralled by their life. They've just gone on a conveyor belt, following the lead and advice of their friends, family, teachers, employers and partners. And somehow they end up flat and dull. Even my father, who's brilliant and has had an extraordinarily successful life, shakes his head and says,

"I cannot believe I didn't pursue music when I was a child." He has this inner desire, and jazz musician friends, whom he's a great supporter of, but you can see how much he wishes he had pursued that creative element and could jam with them. Luckily he was a great sportsman, so he had that other avenue. Mind you, he would have a heap of fun taking it up now.

Creativity is another form of love in action. It's the pure expression of who you are. Being creative makes the world a happier, better and healthier place. I say that creativity's the antidote to heaviness, to feeling lack, to having no imagination and, of course, to being dull or beige. I'm not saying here that you have to take up painting or the arts, or that you need to suddenly become a floral designer or a knitter – although I highly recommend all of these. I'm talking about drawing on what life really is. Life is a never-ending stream of creation and activity. When we're creative, we're building a relationship to access our inner genius.

Creativity is also nurturing.

> 'To get in touch with the core of life, you have to get in touch with the creative power of the universe. That power expresses itself through your personal creativity. When you are in the field of creativity, you lose track of time. Only the flow exists.'
> **– Deepak Chopra**

And now I get to talk about my absolute favourite subject: spanda. Spanda is the divine feminine that I was talking about before, but to be even more exact it is a moment of stillness, when you experience the dynamic stillness of God. When God wills it, he creates, and that first pulsation of will or desire that created the universe is called spanda. Brilliant word. We need it in the English language!

Everything that comes, everything that's created and manifested, first begins with the initial pulsation of the universe and it is sustained by that same pulse, that vibrational energy. This is called the spanda principle.

If you look at my mandala, you can see how spanda works. It moves from the inside out and our job is to utilise the energy to move from the outside back in. Eloquent, yes? Spanda is pure creativity; it is the creative principle. Spanda, or Spandashakti, is the universal artist that's constantly creating and manifesting. It's taking place in every activity in every moment from every thought to every feeling, to every invention, to every action. There are three aspects of God: birth, preservation and death. That is creativity. An idea is born, it has a certain lifespan and then it finishes, goes away, whether it's the galaxy itself or the steam from a boiling kettle. It's a never-ending process and that is what life is all about. Do you see how important it is to create? It is essentially who we are. It is our nature. It is the energy flowing through us. Go with it!

When we don't appreciate the cycle, we don't know to sit back and go, "Okay, that had its time. It had to go." When we think something should be around for longer than it has been, we end up in pain. We are expecting things against the laws of the universe. We are trying to control the universe. This is a form of suffering.

Being creative and in touch with your inner creator is extremely powerful. It empowers us. We draw upon this energy and slip into a stream of consciousness that is beyond thought and feeling. You've probably heard of the sportsman or the artist going into 'the zone', where they don't even realise if they're hungry or need a break. I used to be like that when I was a chef.

I'd work for incredibly long hours, but I was so in the zone with the deliciousness of the activity and the creativity that is cooking and serving beautiful food to nourish people. Now imagine it. Can you close your eyes for a moment and get in touch with your breath? Take a few deep breaths. Feel the rise and fall of each one. Be comfortable and get in touch with your inner world. The closer you go to your absolute stillness the more you'll realise that there is a throb. There's a throb to life, a vibrant pulsation. Now you're getting in touch with the spanda, creation.

How we get in touch with this – what modality and in what medium – is where our true genius lies. I'm an artistic person, a multi-creative, and of all the artistic avenues I've pursued fine art is what lights me up the most. It fulfils me emotionally. I also loved and drowned myself in music to survive being a teenager in an unhappy home situation and dealing with chronic illness. I played the piano, violin and viola. I drew all my early childhood but when I stopped remembering the fine artist in me I became a robot.

At one stage I was encouraged to step away from art. I was a single mother, my children were little and painting wasn't bringing enough money to put food on the table, so people said, "Oh, you're a better cook than you are an artist. You should take up cooking as your art form." So I went and did my chef's apprenticeship. It didn't take long – about a year – until I realised that some part of me was actually dying. It was extremely difficult to get back on that feeling. I love and adore cooking, and being a chef really suited the part of me that is high impact and loves energy, but I'm at my happiest as an artist, a visual artist.

When I was learning how to build my own website during my convalescing period I came across the notion of self-branding. This reactivated the fine artist in me. I was in bliss! I'm fascinated now with 'Self', the highest form of Self-branding, and luckily now here I am. I'm middle-aged, studying graphic design and am adoring using my fine art abilities and new tech skills. As much as I love food and cooking and the thrill of it all, I really am an artist. It puts me in touch with that divine pulse of the universe.

As I said before, creativity is not limited to the arts. It is how we approach life. It is how we relate and approach our families, our careers, our wellbeing and our issues. When we can't be creative, we know that there's a block of energy, that we're stuck. It means we're out of the flow or Tao and can't feel that pulsation. When there's stagnation, which to me is the worst nightmare ever, it means you need to change how you are doing things. You need to reassess what you are thinking, feeling and who you are being. Something needs to be done differently. A new approach must be made and a new perspective gained. You need to take some space and have a clearing, so that maybe everything can drop into place and start happening again.

Sometimes being creative means that you go on a retreat or have a holiday. It's a change of scenery. For others it might mean spending time in nature. I have a girlfriend who, when she's blocked or stagnant, goes and digs holes in the garden and plants flowers. She has the most magnificent garden and is happy, buzzing and flying by the end of that day. She is happiest covered in dirt, working with the seasons and curating her garden to be a delight of colour and fragrance all year round.

## What is the key to living creatively?

This is it, everyone. Are you ready? In a nutshell it is one simple thing: living in uncertainty. Having absolutely no idea what is going to happen next with wonder and awe in the moment. Don't get fixated on money, or getting the right job or house, or finding the right partner. When you're living in uncertainty you're being creative and digging deep into your being. You'll be coming from the blank canvas and your decision and moods are the colours and images. You're doing. You'll naturally have that seluvial space around you to freely choose and create from.

It's in the present moment. When we're really engaged in it our minds become disciplined as we access the creator within. God adores uncertainty because it is when we're at our most open and receptive. We're a little bit raw. We might have fear but we're still moving forward.

One of the worst times for me was when my relationship ended and I had to move. I didn't have the answers to anything. I didn't know if I was going to find the right house or have enough money. I was terribly unwell and couldn't work for a year or two. I had no idea, but my faith was off the charts because I'd started with my purpose and knew what I wanted from my heart's desire. I didn't care because living was exhilarating. The uncertainty and the faith was a potent cocktail for divine guidance. I'd never been more alive, even though I was possibly at the most traumatic intersection of my entire life and physically broken.

Have a chat with fear. Say to your mind, "Look, I know you're going to find every reason to try to protect me. You're going to do what you do: terrify me into figuring out exactly how things will work out. The uncertainty will create a mood and the need to get things done. It will make me perform in ways and be vigilant and alert for expansion of feeling." This is very difficult for control freaks and micromanagers. They don't live creatively, as they're too busy trying to control and compromise themselves. It's a rough road if you have to know everything and control the world around you. It's like living life wading through mud and carrying bricks on your back. What's the point? Perfectionism isn't much fun or very rewarding. The burden of responsibility must be enormous and exhausting.

Have a chat with fear and find a way to be okay with not knowing what is coming. Be all right with losing sight of where you have been. You're now in the ultimate space of creating. Most people can't do this.

My experience and practice have brought me to a new place. If I don't live at all times through my inner creator in uncertainty, on the precipice, on the edge of the cliff I was booted off not so long ago, the universe zaps me. This is the place of pure potentiality that you hear Deepak Chopra talking about.

It's a lot easier if you are naturally optimistic. But this is how to become optimistic. If you're like me and you've just been told that you have to find another place to live, how do you react? Do you react angrily because it's inconvenient or stressful? I don't know where I'm going to move to or whether it will be the same beautiful place. Will my next place be decent? Will it be close to the things I need? Will it have heating and cooling? Does your mind wear you into a state of frenzy and anxiety, or do you think, 'Wow, a change is coming. I'm being called to something new and wonderful.'

The creative principle is at play and it wants something new and good for you. It wants to gently direct you into your heart's desires, to make you step up to a calling because the world really needs what you get out of it. There's something in your soul's evolution here. Can you meet it with faith, trust, a deep breath and optimism? Can you see that you can start manifesting something fantastic even though you can't see it yet? You can start planting the seeds of what you want. You can create with your visualisations and get your feelings about this move in alignment.

The help will come when you live with uncertainty. The money will come. The how will present itself. Don't panic. I'm staggered and have been shown time and time again that unconceivable things will fall into my lap when I completely live in the present moment and then stop depending on other people and stop expecting things to be a certain way in my life.

May I add here that none of this would be possible if I hadn't started where I started here at the beginning of this book: owning who I am. When I owned my independent nature and stopped looking at getting things from others then I took off. Everything began to move around me. It was so powerful.

This leads to my next point. I was talking before about how you can start to create in that space of not knowing. Here we're going to talk about choice. Did you know that choice is karma? It is whether you make a good decision or a bad one. You either follow through or you don't. Either way it takes you closer to God or further away. Can you see that our relationship to creativity is done with every choice that we make? Our life is one hundred percent our responsibility. How we have reacted to situations, how we have created situations, how we have put ourselves where we are – those were all choices. Some may be from a previous lifetime. Accepting what happens as part of our soul's evolution is not just a relief but is full of grace.

We can either be conscious or unconscious. Have a look. I told you before about life being the full spectrum of the artist's palette. You can tell I'm an artist. Now imagine that your life is a giant canvas that you paint upon. But who is painting? Do you stand aside, go into the witness consciousness of the present moment and allow grace to flow through you to create a masterpiece? Or do you manage to control, though you're not really qualified to? You used the wrong colours, you have no perspective and you create a hideous painting.

That's the difference. Do you let grace flow through you or do you come from your lower self? I want you to be really honest here. What are you doing? Take this to your home life. Take it to work. Think of how you deal with your friends and family. Are you creative or are you intense? Are you fearful? Do you complain? Do you think you're funny or are you really bitching about and backstabbing everyone? Are you cynical? Are you sarcastic? Are you worrisome? Domineering? Weak? Do you own your part in this? I hope every single one of you puts your hand up to something because I can. When I forget who I am, which is not often, I see my lower nature come in. But the good news is I'm so onto this work that it doesn't take long – just a split second – to pull myself up. My entire nervous system, my entire way of being, has now adapted to life as a She-Monk.

How do you see everything that you do? How do you react to things? I find the most difficult people to deal with are the ones who like to pretend everything is just fine, thank you. They put up smoke and mirrors and are happy and shiny, but if you sit with them your gut starts wrenching and your heart pounds. You can feel their grief and pain, but they're slyly manipulating the situation so they seem fine. You end up almost sick by the time you leave them and you can't always work out why. When we do a lot of spiritual work we become remarkably intuitive. We can often feel the unspoken words and the deep inner feelings through even the best most adept cover-up. After spending time with someone it's good to check why you feel sad and awful. It might be because you channelled their unconscious feeling. It is not always our own feeling we are carrying!

Are you holding the paintbrush in your life? If so, what is your painting like? Is it bright, light and happy, or is it dark, sad and tense? Did you know this is all your choice? Now I'm not saying that shitty things don't happen. They come out of the blue like giant curveballs. Hell, I've had more curveballs than anybody I know, but that's because I now know I chose this life to burn off a lot of karma. I knew in this life that I wanted to go home and I was given indicators very early on that that's what I was here for. Knowing this makes my handling of what happens much easier. Every opportunity is an opportunity to purify and clean up as I go. Other people don't understand this. That's the danger of thinking that things only go wrong because you put out a certain vibration. That's naïve. There's a bigger game at stake.

We know that choice is free will, a tiny portion of divine will. Choice is about our decision-making abilities, trust, faith, practice and our smarts. It's the only time our personhood comes into play. It is where we're given the joystick. The game starts and goes as long as we navigate the joystick. Then it comes to an end. That's it. The end may be death, but death itself is terribly creative. It's the end of a cycle and the beginning of something new: our return to energy, to consciousness. The game is over. It's time to go home. Rest and restore. It all happens again. Rinse and repeat for the sake of our soul's evolution until we finally get it and realise the self. We are fully and always creating and we're made from creation. We *are* creation. We're sustained by it. Creation is pure spirit and we will die creatively.

Do you get it? Creating is living. It is pure spanda, grace. Therefore it is also mysterious. There's an enormous never-ending tap of inspiration and activity. We can't even think for a moment that just because something is happening to a person it's because of XYZ. That is arrogant. I used to believe that about food. I was told I'd never have children after a lifetime of painful endometriosis. After learning to meditate and moving to a plant-based diet in a time when these things were considered lunacy, I had my two miracle children. After my first child, the doctors said, "Well, congratulations. We don't know how you did it, but you certainly won't have another one." And I did. I had my daughter and then thought I knew the key to everything. Up until my recent ... let's call it ... *sabbatical*, my healing crisis, I honestly believed that you could heal everything with meditation and diet. But you know some things are cosmically organised for us to grasp the laws of consciousness on a much deeper level. We want to be all that. We want to be love incarnate in this world. Things will happen to us that will ground us into that energy so that we can see a bigger picture with more compassion.

It's just like when you're feeling flat and tired at the end of the day in the office. You know you need some fresh air. You know if you dance around and play a bit of music you will start to lighten up. It's the same with life in general. We need a fresh perspective. We need some fresh air. We need to make great decisions and allow everything to flow. If you make a crappy decision, what do you do? Start at the beginning of this book. See why you did it. What was the tendency? What part of your personality? What were your fears? Deeply accept all of it and move on.

This is what it means by being in the world and not of it. That is the key. Stay in that space of detachment and compassion. If the world hooks you in, that's okay; it just means you have to start again.

Finally, mindset is a creative skill. Anything is possible with mindset. I don't want to say you can grow a mermaid's tail if you want to. That is not enough. That kind of thinking annoys me and is a waste of time. I'm saying that by staying in a place of creativity and uncertainty, or pure potentiality, the present moment will show you the road signs and pathways. In a healthy mind, one that creatively handles the lower mind's protective fear and the ego's doubt, these will all unfold. Our lower or the rational mind cannot conceive of the great vastness and tonality in the universe. It is the antithesis to creativity.

So spend time every day outside of that mind, our universal mind. Meditate, swim, walk, dance and laugh. Trust you have the same creative impulse running through you as Mozart, Einstein and Ghandi.

## What if there's no artist within me or I'm not creative?

Simply see it as a metaphor, which is how it is intended. Find something that works for you. You are creative by your very presence here. Simply by being alive you are creative. Where there is life there is creativity. You see things as the artist of your life and you sculpt your life. You go to the inner creator, to your higher self. Paint with the colours you love and wish to see. Create beautiful scenarios and be mindful of what you choose. Your choices are the design of the work.

## How do I become more creative?

The solution to everything is always in the eternal moment. It is in stillness and presence. Meditate. Bring in your divine posse. They're there waiting to help you. Always ask them for help. Delegate what you can't handle. At some stage, ask yourself when you stopped being creative. All children are creative. You just stopped looking for the magic and stopped using your imagination. What did you love doing that you would love to investigate now? Did you secretly want to be a musician like my father? Maybe it didn't work out. Your family had expectations and you became an accountant to earn enough money in the world to have the life you needed. Do you want to save children in detention centres but choose to teach math? Do you wish your meetings were held at the beach instead of the boardroom? There are no limits here. How can you start to enjoy yourself? How can you do the things you wanted to do. How can you take time out from your current thinking and see things a bit differently? How can you go home and let your inner creator show you the way?

## How does this relate to living a domestic life?

There is nothing more creative than the divine mother. No love is closer to universal love than that of a mother. To create a home, a sanctuary, to feed, nourish, care and keep it lovingly is as surrendered and creative as it gets. If that is what your experience is now, then make the most of it. Bring in awareness. Give, give, give and make sure not to lose yourself in it. We're not all meant to be martyrs – ooh another myth!

This also applies in the world (i.e. in your career). Be detached. Do what you need to do, but retreat to your centre, your core, as much as possible until that state becomes dominant. Watch for resentment sneaking in from not giving yourself enough self-love and time off. Being devoted doesn't mean being a slave. Only do it, even if it's home life, if it lights you up. Otherwise go and get help.

Which areas of life need a lift? Get your journal out. Write with a pen and look at the areas of your life that are dull and beige.

Join a group, any group. It could be a discussion group, a book group, a spiritual group, a knitting group or a prayer circle. It could be a comedy club, or a movie-goers' club. It could be a mums and babies swimming group. Join it, get out there, do something different and see the light that it brings you. Whenever you take time out from your usual routine and add colour to the beige you will start to see things differently and find new ways to approach the problems in your life.

Self-love and self-nurture. Can you hear the theme in this book? It is self-love, self-awareness. Make a beautiful home. Find the beauty in nature. Enjoy the arts. I adore the arts. I love how consciousness moves through the artist and they find a way to share it. When you're the observer, simply stand back and you will get a hit of grace or a hit of shakti. The yogis wrote about this thousands of years ago. Even if you can't do, admire. Admire great works of art or sportsmanship. Admire the tremendous feats of human nature.

## *Chapter Ten*
# MYSTICAL WORDS

Mind your language, darling. The words we choose and the thoughts we think determine the quality and experience of our life. Nothing creates suffering and pain for ourselves and others like the use of language. How we express ourselves shows how we are feeling, what story is running and how connected we are to the moment. It shows a resolve to come from the higher Self. When we are open and not blocked, we have amazing self-expression that speaks the truth. It speaks it with compassion because that is how we're meant to communicate.

We speak from the heart and are guided by wisdom. We keep life clean. I have learnt to not sit and wait. If something needs to be said, I say it. If there's some reason to bring something to the surface, I'll bring it up. I'll apologise or do what I need to do if I get it wrong, but I'll always make sure to do my best and keep things clean. I don't take anything away and stew on it, which can potentially make the next communication worse, and I don't leave any situation feeling uncomfortable. That level of commitment and intensity can be too much for people who aren't there yet. We can be so naughty with the language we use. Bringing truth into a room is now one of my most favourite things.

When we change our language, we give ourselves hope. We give ourselves a new perspective and perception of life. We learn to say what we need to say to the people we need to say it to. That is one of my teacher's sayings. Another is 'When the mind moves towards the self it becomes its pure nature'.

> 'There's no desire for those who have no mind. It is our mind that decides value. If the mind is not so disposed, the diamond is but a clod of earth.'
> **– Bhagawan Nityananda**

Isn't that magnificent?

Look at where there is stress, chaos, anxiety and depression. You know these all originated in the mind and manifested through thought and speech. They could be a karmic thing that you have to go through. Sometimes we have to go through things like this. Remember they are a boon, a divine assignment. But if they're ongoing you need to have a look. There's an association. Even though they might be a divine assignment, we can sometimes make it worse. We're feeding the beast when we don't adjust our thoughts, perspectives and language.

This is the meaning of hell. When we haven't been given the skills and don't have the natural inclination or the personality to want to take ourselves home to truth, then we are in hell. Heaven and hell are not physical places. They are both here and now, depending on our state of mind and the language we allow to come from and to us. Admittedly some people are going through horrendous traumas and it is not helpful to expect them to do anything other than survive. But once they are out of that situation and have the ability to heal it's important they go to the source of language.

What we believe and how we perceive it usually dictates how we will respond and react to our reality. Our responses get filtered through our lower or 'manas' mind, which determines whether we live in heaven or in hell. Did you know that language is as mystical as love? It is not solely for the realm of the great poets. Language is an energy. It can express the vibration of love, hate, judgement and discontent. The mind, by the way, is also energy. The tradition of Kashmir Shaivism that I come from says we have three of these energetic minds and the mind is purely consciousness that has been individualised. How cool is that?

This is where we get our individuality from. It's why we think and see things differently and why some of us try to convince others to see things our way. Some people don't realise that everyone has a different perception.

Language is actually alive. It is also spanda. In Kashmir Shaivism, on a basic level, language is said to be made up of matrika, which are these little deities. Letters, words and speech are the vocal manifestation of those deities and they take different sound forms depending on whether there's a good energy or a bad one. Our mind's thoughts can actually affect our biology. The lower mind can cause real damage here. The cells do what they do based on what the brain tells them so if we are constantly thinking bad thoughts we can create disease and dysfunction in the body. To get around this we need to bypass the lower mind and move to the high mind. It's all part of a divine setup. We need to get past the nature of the lower mind, which acts like a shutter to divine intel and truth.

The light is always streaming through, but our perception is our shutter. It's how we categorise and judge things. It determines whether we see light or dark and is part of the concealment of grace. Meanwhile our lower mind focuses only on that which we can interpret through the five senses. Here lies a fabulous insight on how to go home.

My first divine experience, interestingly enough, was purely to do with language. I don't know why or how it happened; it just did. I was eleven years old. It was a gentle warm day and I was walking up the street. I lived in a very beautiful part of the world as a child, right on the beach in a nice neighbourhood of Melbourne. I remember feeling remarkably happy because I've always loved the sun. Suddenly something made me stop and pause. As I felt the sun on my skin I lifted my two arms in front of me and looked at my hands. In that moment, something completely shifted in my being. I got this download. I saw that I'm not the body. I saw that I'm faceless. I realised that these hands were someone else's. I had a complete experience of the witness state and, in that split second, I got a huge download about karma. I was just an

Aussie kid in the 'burbs. I had never heard the word karma – not to my knowledge, anyway. I was only eleven years old, but I was a big believer in magic, had already had divine experiences and loved going to church.

One of the downloads was really fascinating. This internal voice said to me, "Be careful of language. You have tremendous power with how you speak and you must be very careful with it." It continued saying that there is a moment where you can actually catch your thoughts before they come into language. Even if they turn into spoken words there is still a moment where you can erase its energy so it's not as lethal or not as destructive if you let it go. It gave me a way to do that. I had a fantastic experience of the Self. I remember going to school and telling my teacher in an essay about karma. I was absolutely annihilated and humiliated by the teacher. She tore me to shreds and the class laughed. It kind of went underground for me after that. It became my own personal fascination. It was like life became a game and I saw the impact of language. It wasn't until I was sixteen that I heard a teaching that took me to that same level of wisdom, a level I had never heard again after my initial experience.

Language, the spoken word, is the world's greatest tool, or it can be the world's most destructive weapon. Language that is creative and divine sets off an energetic signal into the ethers that attracts magnetically, like energy. Language that is not like that is destructive and attracts similar energy.

I wasn't told in that moment that it's imperative I learnt to quieten my mind. I think it's funny that the universe gave me the most active mind. Seriously guys, if I can do this work literally anybody can. There's hope for all of us.

I used my creativity to quieten my mind as I loved the arts, especially music at that stage; dancing, before my knee deformity interfered; and I enjoyed drawing for hours on end. I would play and create all day every day. It was an emotional release.

Having children was one of the biggest reasons I had to learn to rein in my use of language. There's no greater training ground than having kids – especially teenagers. They are at the most delicate and difficult state in life. Their minds and language can be a little bit off, their self-esteem is so delicate and their ability to process issues and ask for help is running at an all-time low. What we say to them as parents carries tremendous weight and influences them. I noticed how important it was with my daughter as she began to flex her individual teenage muscles. She started, as they all do eventually, to get very moody and angry at times. It was so unusual as she was always so happy, light-hearted and funny. I know she didn't like it either, but the last person she wanted to help her in the world was her mother.

After a few clashes, something in me decided that the best thing I could do was to choose to be a life-affirming influence in her life. I reminded her that she's okay and got her present to the feelings she was experiencing. I'd say, "Oh, honey, you're just in a bad mood and that's okay." I'd get her to own it and be okay with it, even if it was something that she didn't completely understand. I made sure not to say to her, "You're crazy", "You're a loser" or any of those things I was told when I was little. I found that once they go in, they anchor in you and are really destructive. Of course sometimes in the moment I said the wrong thing, absolutely. I'm not perfect. If the wrong thing comes out, you've got to clean up your mess. Have the intention to use language to help keep someone's self-esteem and self-worth intact, like a teenage child, and let them know they are loved and safe and protected as they go through the changes they need.

When we go on and on about our story, our dramas, and we keep offloading our bad thoughts and feelings onto others we're seriously stuck. We're no longer the I AM. I remember experiencing in a meditation once that complaining doesn't only block the energy of the thing you are complaining about, it blocks energy in general. If you're whinging and complaining about how badly your husband leaves the bathroom and then you're expecting something to go well at business … well, you've shot yourself in the foot and made it a lot harder. So don't just think that complaining about one area of life doesn't affect the others. It can be quite harmful to your life in general. Complaining is an incredibly poor use of speech and I love to help people when they come for a session catch their language. It's important for us to own what is so for us in the moment. Although there will be times when we need to offload or vent – hell, I need to vent – but there's a difference between disciplined venting and constant complaining.

One of the kindest things we can do is observe how people catch their awful, awful inner thoughts and inform them that what they're projecting outwardly is simply what they are thinking inwardly. It all starts with what they're thinking about themselves. Pain, confusion, poor thinking, negative language and insecurity makes people bully and inflict pain on other people. That is a poor choice. Remember, choice is karma, which is why we have to watch our language. We want to avoid bad karma because we want realisation. We want to be She-Monks. We want to go home.

My training is to use language as a healing tool. If negativity comes from thoughts and language then the antidote is the same: we must use the right language and have the right thoughts. To acknowledge and change perspective, move to right thinking, use the right language and move our consciousness and energy back up. All this can be done very easily with what is called self-enquiry and we can do it ourselves with practice. It is simple, but we do need to be taught how to do it as, surprise, surprise, we are not taught how to deal with stress, thoughts or emotions at school or growing up. Thoughts and emotions are intertwined, by the way.

Once we learn how to do it ourselves, we can start to do it with ease and mastery. This is the path of wisdom. If someone comes with a really big, unexplainable issue or feeling that they're traumatised, going in there and vocalising what is happening for them is magic.

There are so many forms of self-enquiry. It's not owned by anyone. I have my own form with the spanda mandala and my teacher had a form called the Shiva Process. The most famous is to contemplate 'Who Am I' or the I AM in each and every moment. The beauty of this is it can be done during your day whilst living in the world. Byron Katie has her four-question form. They are all examples of self-enquiry. Experiment and find something that works for you, but you'll quickly see how language and thoughts have shaped your experience. Having the skill at home and in the world is one of the best skills you can have.

Here we are doing God's work. We're being masters of thought and it helps to determine our wellbeing, our success and our happiness. A great place to start is with a compassionate approach to help dismantle the intensity. For example, when my daughter would get moody, I'd say, "I hear you" and I would acknowledge that the way she's feeling must be awful. I'm not fixing it but I'm acknowledging it. Usually that would put down some kind of potential verbal artillery. My daughter is actually the cheeriest, happiest person I know, with the sweetest disposition, so it was really difficult watching her navigate the vicious moods in her mid-teenage period. Luckily it didn't last long.

What we say and think is a choice. Sure there's some unconscious stuff going on underneath. This will come up as we go through the onion layers, as we evolve and heal that subconscious mind bit by bit. But it is not a free-for-all to think nasty thoughts because you can think no one can hear or see them. Don't kid yourself. The universe can hear. You're emanating the energy of it. You're standing there talking to someone, but you're thinking something completely different. You're attracting the awareness of that consciousness. Be very careful of what you create and don't underestimate what a person can pick up. Even an unconscious person. We have little antennae to the unspoken word, it's with the feeling that we can pick up what's really going on.

It is also very important to talk about verbal abuse. There's only so much verbal abuse a relationship can take – aggressive or passive-aggressive; both are hideous. I've experienced both. I had a relationship with someone who was passive-aggressive and it was torturous. I also have a family that were just outrageously aggressive. Passive-aggressive doesn't mean a person has greater personal composure. It can be a sickening control habit and is extremely hurtful. Sometimes I find passive-aggressive harder to deal with because there's just no way you can get around it. They've built this defence system up and if you try to come at it then suddenly you're crazy. I think it's horrible. I cannot stand it when I hear someone say their partner is crazy and the worst thing is if I hear men saying, "Oh, but she's just crazy." Women aren't 'just crazy'; women are highly empathic. They are usually sick and tired of swallowing the misuse of verbal language and thoughts and are desperately trying to resolve the situation. Sometimes they're knocked down because they don't have the tools yet. They don't have that sacred space with their partner to be safe to say what they need to.

Like many others, my family were very vocal. But to this day they have no idea about the responsibility of using language. They used language as a weapon constantly. Both my parents had wounds and had tempers at home, in very different ways. The throwing of verbal abuse, belittling words and dominating language was common. This was seen as okay and normal and, for some reason, it still is. But it's not okay and just because they can't see doesn't make you the weak and crazy one. There's nothing wrong with you – especially if you're brave enough to try to break that cycle. If someone is abusive and have been that way for decades with no remorse or desire to get help or work it out then it is completely all right to walk away from that relationship. You've done your time. Not having control and not being responsible for verbal attacks does serious damage. In varying degrees everyone needs to work on their relationships with the words they use and think. Remember, it starts with a thought, so try to catch it there first.

We need to go to the source of language, which is energy. Work on bringing in or holding grace. At its highest language is truth, or pure chitti, consciousness. At its worst it is a lethal weapon: war. Mantra is the language of the universal mind. It is the best use of language. Mantra has been my life raft. It has taken me to God. It's the canoe that got me across the river, from the bushfire on one side to the peace and serenity of the She-Monk on the other.

Mantra is when you say a sacred word that is alive with grace. You repeat it a certain amount of times, dedicating it to your higher self with commitment. It has the power to bring grace and change in your life. Language coming from a body energised with mantra's divinity is healing. It's transforming. It's true, alive, and carries grace. A She-Monk works to come from this place of infinite truth and to bring that truth to all her communications with herself and others. If I made that sound easy, forgive me; it takes time, skill, practice and connection. This has been a massive part of my life path.

I understood that I was handed intel on a silver platter about the use of language. But still I confess I ended up being someone who didn't always use her speech in the right way.

> 'Reality is beyond speech and thought. Only that which is being expressed in words is being said, but what cannot be put into language, indeed, that which is.'
>
> **– Anandamayi Ma**

## Things that happen to us are caused by the mind?

By our choices, thoughts and reactions. It can be difficult to swallow and difficult to differentiate. We often come from religious backgrounds that teach that God is a man who punishes. When bad things happen we feel like victims or in some way bad. But we are parts of something much bigger, a huge master plan. We can't stop certain events happening, like a natural bushfire that destroys our homes, but we can always consider how we choose to think about it.

We usually don't pay attention to our own thoughts and feelings, or listen to our intuition. When this happens we create some pretty awful and often preventable situations. The best relief I ever got was learning as a teen that we choose our experience before we are born. Some things are a divine setup. We didn't want them to happen so feel frustrated and violated. But we can consciously choose to move to the right perspective. Karma is tremendous like this. We receive the wisdom and love of the divine assignment. Eventually our reactions will become like clouds in the sky and the significance and the meaning will diminish.

## I find it hard to stop self-doubt interfering with my dreams.

Yes, self-doubt is a bitch. I'm very familiar with it. It is present in each and every one of us. If we look at the mandala and the steps of creation, we can see that at one stage we went from being pure consciousness to the energetic signature of a person.

For our souls this wasn't a very pleasant transition and a core wound has hung around with us. yogis call this our Anavamala. Awareness is the antidote. Catch it and become present to the carnage it can create. At some stage we need to learn to work on it, to stare it down, to find the passion and motivation to pull us through negative beliefs.

We also need to blast ourselves daily with what is really true, which is: I am the Self, I am worthy and I am, at my core, wonderful and glorious. Self-enquiry using love-imbibed words of truth really helps. Have a look at trust too. Even with those thoughts, you are still a child of the universe. There is as much assistance and guidance as you can possibly imagine or handle for each situation. It's there. Everything is there for you to build a muscle that's stronger than doubt, so keep at it. Be who you really are.

## My partner and I have some pretty heated arguments. Hurtful words fly out and I always feel terrible afterwards.

This is a commitment issue. This is the manifesto. Both of you need one and now. How much do you want the relationship to grow? You need to overcome these tendencies. If you switch to an intention to heal and stick to your manifesto then you'll eventually turn a corner. You'll both be in a better place to forgive and not take it so seriously. Make sure you both know that one partner's anger and frustration is a cry for help.

We put a lot of pressure on our partners to fill in gaps and find the answers for us when really we should fall more on our communities, healers, prayer and meditation groups, and therapists to help lighten the load. I adore people who get help. They're my favourite beings. We don't have the village communities anymore and families aren't what they once were, so we need to create a support base; we need help. We thrive with community. Humans need it to be healthy and happy.

In meditation spend time becoming aware of your thoughts. Just observe them without any judgements.

Is there an issue that you constantly become stuck on? What are you plugged into? Where do you get angry? Are you holding blame?

Are your words relaxed or are they stressed? Are they stuck in the future? Stuck in the past? Or are they in the present?

Sit with the feeling.

Acknowledge the feeling (e.g. say, "I am stressed").

Investigate what happened – ("I am stressed because…").

"What do I want?"

"I don't want to feel like this anymore."

"I want to feel …"

"I don't know yet how to but if I am consciousness then in time I will."

It's okay to have a human moment.

"I'm moving to embracing and accepting."

"I forgive."

"I can do this."

"I move to positive language, thoughts, feelings, actions."

"I have within me all I need to be grace and graceful right now."

"I am that. I am creation. I am source. I am the universe."

Learn self-enquiry. Sit and contemplate the I AM. Use magical words – words of hope, God and joy. Use appreciation as a vehicle. As soon as you're complaining about something catch it and say three good things that you appreciate.

## Chapter Eleven

# TRANSCEND, TRANSFORM

This is where the soul healing takes place. It is the bigger picture of why we're doing everything that we do. This is the attitude that we're looking for. Experiencing grace as our higher self is often a short-lived experience, one that we consistently try to repeat until we learn how to hold it permanently. The deal is we bring it back, ground it through us and connect with the world again as our higher self.

This magic formula leads us to see everything as grace, as an extension of us. Here we transform the spiritual experience into our world. We don't hang around in lofty, transcendental places, as yummy as that is. We let it become something that grounds us and use it to act out our purpose. I believe that in this period of the evolution of consciousness we are moving away from always looking out for ourselves to wondering how we can use this to help others. Have you ever thought of why so many people are awakening on the planet?

There's a lot of lovely fuzzy stuff out there because we are moving into higher realms and new dimensions, sure, but there is another reason and it is not as pretty. We awaken to help the planet. Remember, awakening isn't enlightenment but if it's a big kundalini one it will take you there. The planet is in the worst shape it's ever been in. I don't mean to be a downer here but I really want to stress that we are creating a mess. Get real and see where we are headed if we keep tolerating the way the corporations, the government, education and the way we do things. We're at a crisis point and it's dark out there. The human spirit is struggling. We are awakening to help lighten the load and help the planet. What are you doing? How are you helping? How many people can you help share your wisdom and experience with to move us towards peace and healing of humanity and the planet? Please don't get caught up in the romance of this window of mass awakening. Get out there and make a difference in the best way you can: by using your genius and purpose. If we miss the window and it shuts, which it could, what will your legacy be?

Transcend and transform! Here is where we gain the right attitude and the right action. We've moved beyond the senses. We have gone home and come back with that home, so we're permanently home. Make sense? Here it's not just about how to be love in the world; it is about how to *be* love in the world.

Sadly, like anything else, spirituality can end up as a front, a simple uniform, unless we are the real tiny percent who actually implement the work. It is no different than any other area of life. It's the same path as an entrepreneur. Entrepreneurs do a lot of study. They work remarkably hard, take a lot of programs and launch a lot of projects, but did you know it's only the 1–2% that keep going and actually succeed at it?

There's no difference in spirituality. Those who remain tirelessly open to the truth of the universe, who melt in the fire of grace, meet the ego, and keep up the wonder and love of the child, are spiritual warriors. They are rare – the one percent, or even less than that. It is one thing to transcend, but it's a whole other ball game to transform. Sometimes we must leave the clinginess, the neediness, of the transcending, the holding onto of the mother figure, the deity, the temple, whatever it is. Even, the bliss of it. We must let go of the side of the pool and swim on our own. I believe this is the fundamental, original work of the monk and the beauty is, from an esoteric point of view, we can do this anywhere and at any time in the world. This is the world of the original rishis.

> 'I have been all things unholy. If God can work through me, He can work through anyone.'
> – **St Francis of Assisi**

When we don't transcend we stagnate, running circles in some kind of never-ending spiritual practice. It can get very, very dry and we can even become disheartened.

When we don't bring down that vibration of love and transform it into our being and world, we're actually missing out. We miss building it, sculpting it and working with it so that our cups fill with grace and love. This is where the cup overflows and affects the world around us, can in fact help fill up the cups of others. When our cup overflows we become fragrant with love.

Hopelessness is an outcome that occurs when we're stuck in a never-ending cycle of just dry spiritual practice. Or it can occur when we get too esoteric. We fly too close to the sun and we get burnt, or go crazy. Other outcomes are wariness, disillusionment, inertia or sickness.

If we don't do this we will never embody that divine love – not at the level we all could. This is all about love. It is about living with devotion, in the truest sense of the word. It's about being of service to humanity while keeping ourselves in the care of grace.

You have worked out who you are. You have drunk at the well, followed the disciplines; done the meditations; and spent days, months or even years sitting in stillness, sometimes in agony, crying to God, asking "How am I going?" and "Why am I not changing?" We're sitting there, not watching our thoughts and purifying our actions. We experience and realise that the true healing, the soul stuff, is beyond the body. It is when we bring back that love. We *are* that love and that love is beyond words. We ground it through ourselves and back to earth. Magnificent, yes?

We don't need to be anywhere. We don't need to be somebody special to do this. There is no longer any other way. The goal of the mystic, the yogi, the She-Monk, is to transcend the limitations of the mind, body and emotions, and to merge with the divine.

Transcending was something I became very good at, but this didn't necessarily mean I could function in the world. One day I became perplexed that I was still experiencing a lot of suffering in my life. I was a great spiritual aspirant. That area was extremely good for me, but my world wasn't great, even though I did a wonderful job juggling study, work and raising two wonderful children. I hadn't nailed the transformation part because my idea of transformation was limited.

I am forever grateful that I had my time in an environment that supported my experience and ecstatic states of grace, but there came a time when it lifted, when it wasn't enough. It wasn't the whole story. I could roll around in blissful states for ages, but there was more out there. The universe made that abundantly clear. I belonged out in the world and yet I had no idea how to make that transition.

I'd been grappling with the bridge between personal development, spirituality and functioning as an empowered spiritual being for some time but did not necessarily want to become too tied up with success language and push. Even though personal development teachers said inspiration was the way, their energy was of push and will which was really the antithesis to what was manifesting in me.

At a Q&A session again at Satsang, somebody once asked what the difference between transcending and transforming was. I really picked up here and listened intently. The answer was a major light-bulb moment of transformation. My teacher paused and then came out with one of the most marvellous explanations I've ever heard. His answer was very simple. I'd heard it many times, but not in this context. He said, "Atma Vyapti and Shiva Vyapti." Vyapti is a Sanskrit word that means integration.

I'd been looking for this nugget and, as happens, grace arrived at just the right time. This one went right down into the soul. I had a transmission of energy as understanding. Atma is another word for our soul. Shiva is the word for God, the formless aspect of God, of pure universal consciousness. He said that transcendence is the Atma Vyapti part and the transformation is in the Shiva Vyapti part. For a mystic, this means we transcend the personal and integrate with the self. That is transcendence. We integrate and have an experience with our God self. Then we take that energy and bring it back down as God – who is Shiva in this instance – and we integrate that into our present, worldly existence. How fabulous is that? Have you ever heard of anything better?

You don't *just* transcend or transform; you need to do both. Put another way, you could say that, after transcending or merging with God, the transformation is when we take the vision or God's perspective back to the world. This is radically different to the world of transformation that I'd experienced that didn't light me up or make me happy. It's like the early pioneers of personal development cottoned onto what these spiritual mystics and yogis were talking about. At some stage they must have spent some time going through the old esoteric teachings and scriptures, but essentially what they've done is shot down the spiritual bird and plucked its eyes out, leaving the carcass to rot. This is why solely doing personal transformation work won't liberate you, though the wisdom you gain will at least give you wonderful expansion, opportunity, growth and success in the world. I highly commend people who go down that path. I think they are fabulous. Part of me also goes down that path. It's who I am.

But you can't take away the consciousness part and expect God. Just like we can't think that veganism or vegetarianism will liberate us faster, or that behaving a certain way or wearing certain clothes will get us to God. It doesn't work like that. You need to know that you are that from the experience of being in that stillness, from keeping your heart open in the world. Keep your heart open in the world!

Go to the direct experience of God long enough and you will start to know who you are. The next step is to then bring that vision back, as you, to the world. Here is the ultimate success, the She-Monk's I AM. This is our goal. Here you graduate, but now you have to accept your life in the world and keep this level of awareness. Sounds easy? God no. Again, many people can buckle here. I certainly took a long time to get it. But it is possible.

Once this happens the next step is to say to the iccha, the divine will that flows through, "Oh my god, how do I serve you? How do I do what you want of me?" We become a servant. This is a fully devotional practice. To me, the grounding of the energy put me back in touch with my natural rhythm on earth and linked all this to my purpose. Purpose as service was the transformation part. Without it I would not have continued to suffer or died from illness.

The transcending part is simply going home. That's why we're here. It's what we're trying to do. When we're depressed, we're desperate to go home. We don't want this feeling of separation. That is all it is. Some of us are so desperate to go home that we become suicidal. Here we no longer identify with the body. What we experience is beyond our senses and physical actions. Here I now had a new relationship with my mandala and tweaked it. It was originally my form of self-enquiry using what I'd been taught (i.e. using language to create a flow of grace and expand our being). Now I also bring purpose in to our highest want. It's very simple and effective. Being a visual and practical person, I need to have it all in the mix. I can't just read about it. I created steps that I can take someone through. They acknowledge and own what they really want, and then, when they finally have it, they see how that feels and how that looks in the world. This vision plants a seed. Often when I create a mandala vision board with people I get them to find a symbol that represents the highest expression of them and put it in the middle of the circle, like this:

This is home.

We find the way out of the perceived struggle, but also come back with a vision to use as a guide. I'd take clients through an understanding and an awareness of the three centres of manifestation, which are: the mind, the heart and our action centre, which you could also call the gut. As we grow in spiritual energy, we transcend upwards, away from the body, to our source self. But grace is also meeting us. Remember, God will take more steps towards us. Shiva Vyapti's rich. Shiva Vyapti is all about love. The analogy of a relationship with a loved one is the perfect training ground for this, for now they are that beloved personified, as is everyone you meet with your transformed view. You are essentially now one.

We are now aware that everything around us is a manifestation of the exact same love that we experience. It's magnificent. People may think you're crazy. You could be in the supermarket and see someone, see how precious and magnificent they are, and it just tears you up because they don't see how wonderful they are. There are so many beautiful souls in this world. I love and adore the normal person, just your regular person down the street. Meeting people lights me up and makes me very tender. I'm sure they look at me like I'm not quite right.

Our jobs, kids, homes and partners are all the unique expression of divine love. Here we sit in wonder and awe, where we understand the true meaning of devotional texts. I know that my illness, my healing crisis, was part of this. Nothing could have grounded me quite like it. Having this understanding – which, again, I thank my teacher for – relaxed me so I could let everything take care of itself. Sometimes awful things happen. That doesn't mean you're a failure! You may be blessed. These experiences are here to ground us deeper into ourselves and give us the kind of knowledge the universe wishes us to have, knowledge we wouldn't otherwise get. We have the wrong way of looking at things when they go 'wrong'. We see these negative things and our fear mind reacts accordingly. Embrace what you are going through. I know it's hard and that some things are truly hideous but if you want to heal and live and thrive this is the way.

I also found that consciously earthing was beneficial and helped with the transformation part. Keeping our feet on the ground and being in connection with Mother Earth helps keep me grounded, as does spending as much time as possible in nature with my bare feet on the ground or being in water by the beach or in lakes. My favourite river is at my dad's rural property in the high country. It runs right past the front of the cabin. Whenever I'm up there I am recharged. It's a free healing session! Back at home I have a few soft, rounded river rocks. I put them between the soles of my feet when meditating and have found that grounds me too.

> **'If you think you're enlightened, go spend a week with your family.'**
> **– Ram Dass**

How cute is that? It's so true. Even though you see the world of love, it doesn't mean you won't be snagged by people or situations every now and then. It takes a little while for our nervous systems to catch up and align with who we are. Don't beat yourself up if you fall behind. Reactions will move quickly through you. Others may think you're a fraud or failure, but you don't care anymore because your eyes are on your purpose and vision and you see them as sparkling lights of consciousness.

### I find it difficult to move beyond the body and transcend, let alone transform.

It takes time and practice for all of us. Find a wonderful yoga or meditation practice. You can start with the body. Have regular communion with it. Talk to it, hear what it has to say, what it has been storing. You can have a transcendental moment by doing this! Create the space for it to happen. Embrace your body and work on what keeps you stuck. Figure out what tendencies you have that are not preventing you from letting go and move towards your highest self. That's where a lot of mindfulness practices start. It is possible to have an out-of-body experience too early. That can be very traumatic. There is an opportunity, a window, to climb through and experience a different realm of being, of consciousness. In the text *Spanda-Karikas* scholar Jaideva Singh says that you can have an eternal moment, a moment of grace, a snapshot of God simply by sneezing. Think about that. During a sneeze you pause everything for that split second. Sneezes are larger than life. You will now never look at sneezes the same way!

I use mantra repetitions. I was very busy but unwell. To get what I wanted, I tended to overrun my body and ignore its needs and limitations. I later learnt that the body was the last thing I focused on, but it eventually set me straight by totally shutting down ... twice. I learned from that 'massive action' or doing that no matter how inspired it is it is not what this body wants! It's not for everyone, though every part of me enjoyed it and saw it as the only way. I was also ignoring another huge part of me: the part that loved rest, recreation and stillness. My belief system had conditioned me to see this as a weakness. Now it is my strength! My knees are disabled and, as a result, I have arthritis. When I'm older I may get two knee replacements, though living with my perceived limitations has given me knowledge and wisdom, which I can now share with you. Now I sit here and appreciate them and tell them how beautiful they are and lovingly touch them with immense gratitude.

Practices like Hatha Yoga are designed for this. Find a local yoga class and join it.

Mantra is a great way to pause everything around and inside of us. It gives that overwhelmed and overloaded mind of yours a rest. Once you get the mind out of the picture, the body can then present itself. Everything can present itself. Anyone can meditate. If they say they can't it's because they haven't found the right technique or they haven't stuck it out to break past negative habits. Mantra repetition is the bomb here. I can't recommend it highly enough. If you want to transcend, find a mantra and repeat it with dedication everyday. Exercises like dancing, swimming or running can help.

## How do I hold all this love in the moment when things are difficult?

Practice! Find the divine right perspective and language. Don't worry about it. It's the intention that matters. Try to move to the witness and watch the trigger points, the values and beliefs of yourself and others. Take notes. Make it an experiment. There's always going to an Achilles' heel or personal kryptonite. It just takes time. Difficult situations are training grounds. Without them we'd become complacent and fall asleep. We need to keep doing what we can do to prevent our cups from cracking and our leaking energy. Go through this book again and keep up the practices. You will get divine intel and intuition. Get help too! Not enough people get good help, which is crazy.

Family and close friends know how to get to you. Have you noticed that no matter what you do to reinvent yourself family always see you a certain way? Maybe they're basing this on something you did when you were three years old. To them you will forever be that person. It's a lost cause. Be love as much as you can. You'll see that the more you work on yourself, the better the effect on your family.

Some people might even have to leave their family. This is extreme but in some situations it is necessary, especially if our families are preventing us from being the best versions of ourselves. Even family can, in extreme cases, be destructive and unhelpful. They can be cultish, clannish and are usually in denial because their habits and attitudes are so ingrained. Eventually we will reach a stage where we rise above and break the cycle of destructive and co-dependent relationships. For some that can be our life's work. This can show up in relationships in various ways. Healing is part of our soul evolution in this life. Do the best you can and do whatever it takes to be what you most want.

It takes time and practice to build the muscle of tolerance and compassion and to hold a space in difficult situations. Just think about you. Remember, this is about the vision and how we see the world. Try to see sparkling, glittering rays of divine energy in it.

Spend time asking for divine assistance and as much grace and mercy you are able to receive. Prayer works a treat in difficult situations. So does letting go and surrendering and, most of all, being spiritual doesn't mean taking crap! Not at all. Find where the good feeling is, the expansion in your options, and go there.

On another note, ask yourself honestly if you are having a tantrum because what is happening isn't what you want? You'll be surprised at what comes up. That may lighten your load, allowing you to start moving towards peace and healing.

## I don't think I can do this at work. It sounds too hard.

Maybe at this stage. After reading this book and taking on its suggestions I'd be surprised if you remained at a job that caused you grief. I'd hope by then that you'd be doing something that lights you up. Remember, you can accept the situation, change the situation or you can leave it. Don't spend your entire life at work trying to change the situation if it's just not going to happen. If it's not lighting you up, look at what you want.

In this day and age, you don't have to stay in a crappy place with negative people. Do you love what you do? Is it your purpose? Do you wake up with excitement and enthusiasm? Take it step by step. A great place to start is to stop complaining and look at your expectations. Take on the idea of seeing your bosses and colleagues as love and see what happens. You may need some time off – a home retreat perhaps – to get a fresh perspective and renewed energy.

What shift in perspective can help with this work-related fear? I'd recommend some self-inquiry and gratitude and go from there. You can sit there and adore them for who they really are and you can have compassion for their humanness.

Find someone who has transcended and transformed. Likewise with personal development and business. If you want to succeed and transform it's best to hang around people who have done this themselves. I'm not saying become them or get roped into doing things that you know are wrong. I'm saying look at their formula and try it on for size. By doing this your own formula will reveal itself, which you can then share with others.

Make sure you have a spiritual community that supports and encourages the delicate, subtle movement of the spiritual energy. We can't do this alone. You can't be in the world as a single pioneer and expect to have that grace – unless you are destined like Ghandi. Though look what he had to go through. It won't happen. You have to build up the energy. You need support. If you want to stay in a monastery-like community, that's sensational. Or maybe you're like me and you feel a strong calling to be independent and take your spirituality to the world. I know I need a spiritual community and like-minded people to connect with. I have created my own.

Find people who will reflect love and help you come back to the right understanding. They should be compassionate and know who you really are. Remember, this is about the heart. Don't leave anyone out. A bird can't fly with only one wing. We need all our parts: the heart, the mind, the body. This is all about love and how to integrate everything back into love.

Love, think well and do good things. Choose to be a good person, someone who's honest and transparent and centred on others. And, of course, you can always come away on a retreat with me!

Transcend – practices that take you to God.

Transform – bring that awareness back down through you and ground it to a universal vision.

## Chapter Twelve

# HOME TEMPLE

Home is our sacred space. Not some little spot in the corner that we designate our sacred altar; our *entire* home. We expect the spiritual energy we are building and nurturing to fill up every room. Our home is a sanctuary for ourselves, our family and anyone who sees it. As soon as someone walks in the door, they can feel that release of the strain and stress of the world. Home is our temple.

All the tensions leave when people come in. They can sit down, relax and experience the serenity, the work, the meditation and the love. Some can even move to an altered state. No matter their personality, children are very happy and always obliging, I've found, to honour the sacred space. Our home is the monastery and we are the creative directors of it.

If we are love in action in the world, our homes need to support and represent that. Home is where we nestle, plug in and recharge. We need it desperately if we want to pull off this She-Monk business. It's a place that invites joy, rest, meditation, peace and harmony. This is self-loving, nurturing.

We don't do enough of that.

By the way, I'm not saying go Zen, unless you want to. Minimalism actually disturbs me! You can be as colourful and as *you* as you wish. The deal, as Buddha says, is everything in moderation. Our home is our temple. We don't have to leave. We honour who we are.

When we keep the spiritual energy in the one place, we have assurance that if something happens, if we knock ourselves off course – say someone in the car park runs into your new car with a shopping trolley – we at least know that we can go home and enjoy that lovingly built up, relaxing energy as soon as we walk in the door.

The home temple is where we look at doing home retreats. Three or four times a year, I clean the house up and get it ready for a home retreat. I found I got just as much, if not more, from being silent in my own space than when I did so elsewhere. The home temple is a place of healing. We rest and let ourselves rejuvenate. And what about beauty? Beauty is an attribute of the divine. It can be a soul's want.

I don't want a Zen home. Is that surprising? I want a beautiful home, one that, for me, is like an artist's retreat meeting a nature spa. You know what? It's easy too. What fascinates me is how dull the average house is. No wonder people are grumpy and cross! They don't care about their space or understand what it can be. Its only function is to serve as a place to eat and watch the TV. There's no sacred intention.

Since we got rid of the sacred in society, many of us are losing the art of living and having a home and a family. Homes aren't just some impersonal space to recharge our phones and have the odd sleepover. We don't *live* in our homes anymore; we just impersonally inhabit them.

In Australia we now have enormous homes, which many of us get lost rattling around in. We've forgotten what it's like to live and we've forgotten how beautiful it is to be close with others.

Don't miss the potential to create a fulltime spiritual retreat, a place of rest and beauty that is your own home.

This is a fun part to self-love.

> 'Imagine yourself sitting in a perfect, comfortable spot for meditation. It might be a chair in your bedroom or living room. It is a place of relative quiet and calm, somewhere you go on a regular basis to find the peace that only God can give. You have come to realise that the time of rest, in its stillness and peace, is beneficial to both your mind and body. You've come to surrender to God, using a prayer or mantra to move beyond the frantic and overwhelming thoughts that stalk us night and day. You're making a pilgrimage home, where your life will be renewed.'
>
> **– Marianne Williamson**

Isn't that beautiful? When we don't build a home retreat, we start looking outside of ourselves for retreat. We only switch on when we go on somebody else's retreat and say, "Oh, that was nice. Oh damn, I'm back at home." Can you see how crazy that is? Don't put the grace and shakti for everyone to benefit from somewhere else. If your home isn't aligned with your highest values, how can you get that deep communion that you need? How can you get that quiet time needed to be still and be with God?

When my house is in disorder, when it isn't beautiful and full of love, I become scattered, anxious and down. Many people feel this way and have no idea how simple the solution is.

This disorder does not match you being a She-Monk. It's inauthentic to be a She-Monk and not love your space – not when everyone who comes over says, "Oh, I love it here. I feel so good." We can spend so much money and time running away from home if we are so stultified, either playing video games or zoned out in front of the tele. When she got older my mother would be gone from dusk till dawn. She couldn't handle being at home. She also didn't have much room to do up her home, which was the one thing she wanted to do. She wasn't independent like that. I used to feel for her. The worst thing was that when she died my father did the work on the home that she had desperately wanted. Don't waste your time by not having a beautiful home now. Even if you have little money, you can always do something. Bring out your resourcefulness and take the project on.

We also need rituals to come back. Celebration and rituals, like sitting down to dinner with others or lighting a candle in prayer, is part of the juice, the fun, the stuff that we and our children will remember.

Remember, as She-Monks we're all about spirit first and world second. Our living space needs to reflect this too. Temple first and the world second. We need a place to unhook and create the sanctuary that is necessary for self-love and meditation. In essence, our home is an extension of our practice. It's about holding the grace, about being restful, peaceful, artistic, beautiful. For others it may be something else. I have a library full of books and adore them. Don't take my books away just because they're considered cluttered! Sure, don't clutter, but don't have bare-boned rooms either. I don't want to live in a hotel room; I want to live in a home. That's my personality.

I also believe that walls are there to have artwork on. My kids and I are artists. I don't get walking into a place that has nothing on the walls. Although for another person this might be the right vibe. It's all about how you rest and restore. Your home should be a natural expression of who you really are. That's all that matters.

The good thing about making your home a monastery is we can take on the schedules and disciplines needed to be healthy and happy in that home. Part of health and wellbeing comes from participating in the upkeep and maintenance of that space.

In the past, the deal was you move to the Himalayas to concentrate on spiritual practice. If that is what is naturally flowing through you, if it is authentic and congruent, then by all means go for it with everything that you have. But a lot of people end up leaving their homes and families to do that thinking there is no other option. Really consider if it's necessary.

Back then, having a job and family was all-consuming. It took the focus away from the practice. But we're now at the stage in our evolution of consciousness where, with the right intention, the right effort, and by finding the space, the personal time and inspiring those around us, we can, in fact, do it all and be in the world. It is all one; there is no separation. The skill is to make it one. Being the best you in the world won't work if you don't have a place to withdraw and restore. You will get exhausted and give up. Managing our energy is vital.

As a She-Monk, you have an enormous amount of spiritual energy. This energy is often a lot for other people to handle. If your partner also has a massive energy personality consider that you may need your own sanctuary, your own rooms. To be successful in a relationship you need to have your own space and independence. You find this with celebrities and very successful people. They know that they have to have complete alone time. I applied this in my last relationship. The two of us had big energies and we realised very early on that we had to have our own rooms. It was a brilliant setup. You became really keen and eager to see that person the following morning, and you could always have sleepovers. Think about it. You have your own room and that is your mega sanctuary. No one shares that space. Not even your children, unless they are invited. Everyone has their own. It's where I am with myself. I love my own space; I love my own room.

To run your own home as a She-Monk, consider these three fundamental non-negotiable areas. They might surprise you. First of all, another lost art of living and wellbeing is the amount of people who no longer know how to cook. To be empowered, healthy and to thrive we need to be mindful of everything that we do. Not knowing how to cook throws us out. We need to eat nourishing food: the right food for the right season at the right time. People no longer know how to treat and prepare many foods. They think they have food intolerances but that's not really it at all.

I am a spiritual chef, a health coach and for a while I ran my own business called The Yoga of Food, which initially started with spiritual cooking. I soon discovered that most people can't even cook rice properly. I was shocked. These were home cooks. I also discovered that the many dietary theories out there have put people off. We are overwhelmed and overloaded with opinions and studies. Even I was bamboozled. In the end I couldn't stand any of them. Even I was lost and confused – and I'd taught for years!

I had to go back to my roots. That's when I realised that very few people know why they eat what they eat. We're in a decline because of that. Our natural instincts and connection to the earth has been lost, which means we no longer know what foods are seasonal, local, what needs to be raw or what needs to be cooked. We don't know to listen to our digestion, chew our food slowly and breathe while we are chewing.

Many people don't realise that the spices in Indian food – the original stuff; not the chicken tikka masala you get in your local restaurant – were there for medicinal purposes. The cuisine was part of their Ayurvedic medicine system. In India, the spices were at one time prescribed for health benefits. Gorgeous, isn't it? But this is fast becoming a lost art form, even in India. There they consider the seasonings, the balance, the taste, the bitterness and sweetness, and the smells. They are so spiritually connected to food over there, like nowhere else. The reason they eat with their fingers is to keep the connection to the earth, to consciousness and to spirit. To them, utensils break the connection. It's terribly mindful. Have a go.

Cooking, to me, is self-love in action. It wasn't unusual for the head of a monastery or teacher to tell aspirants to learn to cook by themselves and eat alone. They needed to do that as part of their progress. I thought this was touching and beautiful. They were teaching people who had always had someone else do it for them how to self-nurture. This basic practice puts you back in touch with your humanness, which I find so grounding.

We end up creating our day out. We do anything not to have to cook and then rush around saying, "I don't have time. I'm not in the right state of mind. I can't even prepare." We have households full of people and yet one person does all the work. It's crazy! These massive new homes in Australia and I'm sure other countries now have massive huge kitchens. Everyone has to have a huge kitchen. Chefs don't even get the space that the average domestic cook now has and still they don't do that much healthy cooking. Crazy.

Another important part of cooking is learning how to grow food. If you have a balcony it takes nothing to put out a pot and grow some herbs. Start simple. In a backyard you can grow simple things like lettuce, tomatoes and cucumbers. It gets your hands dirty, gets you back in nature, and gets you back with the cycles and rhythms, the spanda of nature.

Something magic happens to you. If you're allergic to food and have dietary requirements, get proactive. Get a handle on discovering the nutritious healing repertoire of food. Go out and find a health coach in your area. If you're a celiac, there are beautiful chefs out there who make stunning food who could teach you. You don't have to fall back on pasta and horrible gluten-free bread. There is life beyond allergies.

What I love about cooking is that it uses all the elements. Air, water, fire, earth. Look at the fire in cooking. When man started cooking, and not just eating raw food, he evolved. This is one of man's greatest evolutionary points. In Ayurveda they love the fire because the fire of cooking represents the fire of Agni, or digestion. It's alchemical. You can transform foods from harsh to highly digestible. Lightly cooked foods are simple, quick and if you are busy they're the way to go. Predominately eat plant-based foods. Know what you're choosing. Are you eating stuff that is laden with chilli or salt, is it deep fried? Is it takeaway food, which is going to impact your energy? That's putting holes in your cup. In the long run it's costing you physically, mentally, spiritually.

You don't have to become a master chef.

I really enjoy the *Master Chef* show and think it's been an incredible benefit to Australia. We've gone from being an outpost of British food to a food fusion nation of amazing cooks. Though we eat takeaway and packaged food more than ever, I've noticed that many of the people who do cook stress themselves out thinking they have to make master chef-quality meals every night. Let's just go back to basics: basic, healthy meals, the daggy stuff. Unfortunately this has become so daggy that we can't even tell someone we had baked beans on toast for lunch.

Eating is a major part of mindfulness. It's an act of gratitude and appreciation. It shows how incredible and abundant the earth is, how that food nurtures us and helps us grow, how it feeds our body. Everything comes from the food we eat. It influences our thoughts and actions.

Have you tried eating in peace, in a nice setting, leaving yourself plenty of time to do so? Start and you'll immediately see the benefits. Whatever happened to smelling the meal? Making the meal look appealing? Whatever happened to spending time to focus? We need to slow down, chew, breathe. We need to seriously get back to appreciating food. And you know what? This is laden with grace. Is this making sense?

Here is another non-negotiable. I'm going to call it the Sabbath. Whatever happened to the Sabbath? When I was a little kid, we had five days that were spent either working or at school. You had one day to do all your shopping, play sport and catch up with your friends, and then you had Sunday. I don't think my family knew why but Sunday was the day when everyone did absolutely nothing. Nothing. Sometimes you were so bored out of your brain that time stood still, but it was refreshing. It made us resourceful and creative. You could go back to work or school on a Monday with renewed energy and a clear mind. But something happened along the way. We became 24/7. This has stressed out our nervous systems, which are still ancient and still need that rest. We are pumped, on alert, and we are expecting a lot of ourselves and beating ourselves up all the time. I believe that by shunning religion, we've managed to throw away some of the most fundamentally important needs for spiritual and human welfare.

Think about this. We're not meant to be active 24/7. We're meant to have time off. The Sabbath is a forced retreat. We've thrown it away because we can't stand religion anymore, let alone being forced into anything. We throw it away because we find it inconvenient. We want to do things. We *have* to do things. We blindly do things. We have no time. We're hysterical. We're addicted to doing, to thinking. We can't slow down. We wonder why we do more and more. We're exhausted. As She-Monks we must come back. We must bring back the Sabbath.

It is time to rest and restore and to do so consistently. The body loves consistency. So does grace. We need a day where everyone knows it is quiet. It is time to go within and spend time and communion with God, to enjoy some peace with family before stepping back into the world again. Kids can play and go in the backyard. It is not your job to be an entertainment unit seven days a week. It's good to teach every member of the family to fend for themselves and find something fun to do.

I brought back the Sabbath, or day of rest, in my home. Sunday is a day of reading, sunshine, rest and sitting with my family. To my delight, my children are drawn to Sunday at home like bees to honey. For a while, it was a necessity. Sure, I had to work seven days a week until I had an adrenal breakdown and the kids … Well, they thought they were okay.

Since I was always working they were always off playing with friends and finding ways to entertain themselves. The beauty of a breakdown stage for adrenal crisis is you learn to go back to what matters. For me, that was my time off. It reminded me there is no rush and all I need will come if I simply work on my being and honouring self-love. When I create that space, my children now join in and savour it. For the first time they want to be at home. They want that rest and love the energy I've built in the place. I've seen the difference it makes in them and I've seen the difference it makes in our attitude – even towards dreaded winter! I create the most beautiful winter home, so now, believe it or not, winter has become our favourite season. It is warm and comfortable. I set up beautiful lights and play beautiful music. Winter has become a really joyful, peaceful, nurturing time.

There's more to it too. With the Sabbath comes a detox. Did you know that we have over 40,000 chemicals in our system and environment post World War II? It's not just the antibiotics and the vaccines. We are bombarded by everything through our air and water, to our food, to the chemicals that are in our household furniture. We are struggling to keep on top. We are having allergies, autoimmune disorders, diseases – everything you can imagine – and yet we're not detoxing. We think detoxing is for hippies with their green juices, or for lunatics. Oh my god, we need it. Our bodies need a break as much as our nervous system and our doing centres need a break. Our gut needs a break. We need a day of light food or even just liquid. Our metabolism needs a regular rest as well.

We are designed as humans to have a break from overloading our bodies with three or more meals a day, especially now with the type of food that we put in it. We need to give our digestive system a break to restore and heal, particularly while we have quiet time. This is when we start to access spirit and our own healing capabilities, brilliantly. Our best communion comes on these days. They are days of lightness. No wonder I love the word Sunday. Let's get it back in the sun, the light. Even in the middle of winter. I'm talking about the light of the Self. That's the sun of grace and awareness.

It's important to detox from the digital world also. I turn off the TV and switch off my phone. I don't go on social media. Okay, I'm not very disciplined there; I'm a little bit addicted! I have to work on that. But I try to take a break from anything that is extroverted and outward bound. My children and I find ourselves fresh. I get so much inspiration. Sometimes by Sunday afternoon I'm writing like a mad woman, getting all these fresh ideas and new perspectives. You see, the creativity comes from the break.

This leads me to the word 'convalesce' or 'convalescing'. Does anyone even remember what that word means? Because of my nature and the way I was brought up I believed convalescing was something for weak people. And yet, because I was overworked, trying to make everybody happy and not living my purpose, I of course walked into an adrenal breakdown. Actually I had two in five years. One day I found a great integrative medicine doctor and I said, "For God's sake, what do I need? Please tell me. I'll do anything. What am I missing here?" She said I was now doing everything right, but I had not yet learnt the art of convalescing. Light-bulb moment! I hadn't integrated my worldly life and my spiritual life. I had two different modes of operation going.

This was something I hadn't expected to hear from her. It reminded me that I'm a great lover of Jane Austen, and that I always used to think how amazing it was that her characters would have all these leisurely weekends and walks in the garden. If one of them became sick they'd be wrapped up and looked after. Everyone was always looked after somehow. Back in the day we had connected families and people were sent to healing places to convalesce in a spa or sanatorium. It's so sad that we're losing that. Only ethnic families seem to have maintained that family connection, where everyone is there for each other.

There was a period, though, when we were really present to the fact. Not just the Sabbath or the day off. When something was wrong or we had illness we weren't pumped through the system and quickly thrown out the other side with a prescription. We were given the time we needed to gently convalesce. It was natural. If someone was exhausted, if someone was getting over a disease, they'd go through a stage of convalescing. We have lost that art. We are now on permanent alert and never switch off. To this day I still see this tendency in me. I'm a very passionate person. I love life and I love people, and yet what a joke that nature's way of getting me to look at myself was to take away my vitality. It was the perfect setup. Can you see the divine assignment? Massive doing or action works for some people, but it's not for everyone. This formula doesn't work for me, even though I enjoy it. The more spiritual practice I did, the less doing was relevant for me. Finding balance showed me that I had none. I was all go and felt guilty about taking time off. For my healing, I had to learn to accept that the art of convalescing was totally unfamiliar to me.

My father, used to say that illness and rest was for wimps. He was hardcore and perfectly designed for his successful corporate career. Here I was, a highly empathic, sensitive, creative and spiritual child. My physical and energetic bodies desperately needed rest, creativity, and to be okay to need rest. They needed for rest to be acceptable and civilised, which it is. This is not my fault or my parents'. It's just part of something I was born to get. Does that make sense? I'm not blaming anyone here. They did the best job they could. They were being authentic with themselves to a point. They could've never possibly known what that meant.

Luckily for us, Sunday, or any day of rest you choose, was beneficial for us. But as a teen life got a busier and we started doing what everyone in the Eighties did: filling our diaries. We filled them with everything from football, to ballet, to horse riding, to sailing. Suddenly we had four or five different activities on a weekend. I don't know how that happened or why we thought it was good, why it would benefit kids. Perhaps it's just because we can't sit still with people anymore. It's crazy and it feeds this beast of busyness. I don't think it's a good thing to have children fully occupied seven days a week. Let them rest and be bored!

Some days we were so bored out of our brains that we thought it was the longest day of the week. But I also recall that my brother and I played on the beach, where we were fortunate enough to live. We played in ways that we don't see kids playing anymore. We bonded. Still to this day we talk about how we used to make tunnels in the sand dunes and how we pretended to be pirates. Once video games came in and we got a little bit older, that stopped. We became zombies sitting on the sofa until I couldn't stand it anymore and I decided to switch off. He kept going. Then retail became 24/7 and we all worked on those potential rest days.

I missed the creativity, playful energy and problem-solving that happens when you're mind-blowingly bored. I missed it so much that I literally took a ten-year detox from television. It was brilliant. Half my living room became an art studio and, even when the kids were babies, we all painted and drew instead while listening to lovely music.

The third non-negotiable is a home retreat. Eventually something inside me wanted the silence you get on retreat. I was strongly compelled to find that presence alone and to build up that energy at home. This became a lovely project and experiment. I designed it as if I was organising and running a retreat in a centre somewhere and included all the things that really mattered to me, like a detox.

If the children had an invitation to go somewhere for the weekend, or friends could take them, I'd set it up at least a month in advance. I'd get the house clean, declutter and organise my meals. Luckily I'm a chef, but anyone can do it. If you have a juicing machine and know how to cut, chop and cook, you'll be fine. I didn't want to spend money or have to go to somebody else's place. The trip there, dealing with other personalities, finding the routine, getting up really early in the morning and going to bed late at night, eating at different times. All of that exhausts me and I don't find it beneficial. At times I've even found it stressful. After a trip reintegrating into my world was like crossing over international time zones. It wasn't easy and worse: sometimes in resettling after a retreat I would lose a large amount of spiritual energy.

My home retreat was based around what was good for me. It was all about me. The kids loved it because they were organised and had a bit of a change of plan as well. I'd pull out the phone and wouldn't answer the door. I let everyone know what I was doing ahead of time and kept them informed of my schedule. I'd have some pamper time booked and even included things like massages if I wanted it. People could come to the home and I'd have time to read spiritual texts or books on the lives of saints. Or maybe I'd watch a YouTube clip in the evening of a good spiritual teacher. I love spiritual stories too. They nourish the soul. But please don't take things like scriptures too literally. They're usually allegorical. Once you've experienced an awakening you can read them at a higher level and understand. Then scriptures will be imbibed with a whole new level of understanding and meaning. I would have time for yoga, juices or whatever. It was the ultimate diet for me and I'd be gentle on myself. The rest of the time I would sit and meditate.

Once a year, I would go back to the ashram and have a week-long retreat. It's a great place to plug in. I don't do that anymore as I run my own retreats, but I highly recommend it as it is still very important to go away somewhere different. We need to have different experiences and deepen practices directly from a good and trusted source. We are tribal so get out there when you can. For me, once a year for a big event is great; for others it might be more than that. Either way, connecting with others to make a collective consciousness helps the healing on the planet. We receive divine intel and good feedback when in a group of likeminded dedicated beings.

Another fundamental area to being a successful She-Monk is sleep.

Look, if you're busy and active in the world you need to sleep. Sleep is when we rejuvenate. Most of us aren't getting enough deep sleep because of things like Wi-Fi and late hours. Our circadian rhythms are out of balance. We are inside so much or so robotic in what we do that we don't even know when the sun goes up or down. It's crazy.

If we don't sleep and look after ourselves, how do we expect to thrive? Yes, the cave yogis up in the Himalayas, the monastery, didn't need so much sleep. That's what happens when you meditate all the time: sleep becomes less necessary. But if you're a working mum, or a stay-at-home mum, or you're entrepreneurial you need sleep to restore. Not only do we need daily meditation, inner time and a Sabbath to detox, we need sleep.

Can you hear how important the balance is? I learnt that for every output I needed equal input. The input was rest and lots of good quality sleep. I had never understood rest. In fact, I had so much energy and other people couldn't understand how I could do as much as I did. Eventually, though, I paid a price for this. I started to live off pure adrenalin and had disconnected from my body. I never slept either. I'm not the only one. Fatigue and insomnia is an enormous issue in the world today, particularly in the West.

The harder we work, the longer the hours. I don't really think this is making life better or easier, even if we have bigger houses and cars. We're chasing fear, not a lifestyle. We're scared of being broke, not having the 'stuff', of getting left behind or even becoming homeless. We think there's only one model of doing things. Sure, success equals consistent dedicated action, but the action of the purpose, which is the pull, means everything will be taken care of for you so long as you are mindful and committed.

When I had my healing crisis I knew that spirit was calling to me to do a long period of inner work. It was a Sabbatical. Some could have called it a dark night of the soul, but I don't get too into that. It was simply a sabbatical: time for me to completely pull away from the world. This might come up for us at some stage. I couldn't work, or run the household anymore. I was literally forced to be still. For someone like me I needed it to happen that way. The universe took care of it for me. If it happened to you, don't forget that you'll never go without. Going into a sabbatical is moving into uncertainty. Everything will be okay. I couldn't work for eighteen months but then I decided to build a career. I listened to my intuition and my blobs of light.

We all need a posse of people who are supportive, connected and broadminded. Healers, therapists, specialists, service providers that we know and trust. Get the best people you possibly can. These are guides and angels and helpers in disguise, in human form. Let their presence guide you when you're in communion. If you can be patient and sit in stillness, then you will get the message of who is in your area or who to contact. Wait for the answer. You might find you open up the paper and there's the right person. You might get a phone call. You might realise that you forgot an appointment at some stage.

### I really dislike being at home and cleaning.

Hey, I'm not saying, "Remember, you have to be a domestic goddess." I've been one, but that wasn't where my soul was. In fact, after awhile I couldn't stand it. I remember mopping the floors one day when the kids were babies and having a *The Scream* moment. I felt like the painting by Edvard Munch. But I took it on as my job while I was in that period of my life. You don't have to be good at cleaning your house. No matter where you reside, that space needs to be sacred and honoured. Being messy, or being unwilling to hire a cleaner for help, will only disturb your meditation. I do also want you to see the benefits of a good attitude towards loving service to your home and family if you have them. Sometimes we have to roll up our sleeves and get it, whatever that may be, done to keep harmony and peace of mind.

Incidental exercise is what our bodies are made to do. We're not made to go to the gym for intense sessions then to sit during the day in an office. Our body just wants to move. When I was on sabbatical, I was disabled and very unwell. I had to hire a cleaner and became accustomed to this. Now that I love my work cleaning has become a time waster for me, so I still occasionally hire a professional cleaner. I still choose to do some jobs, though, because they create a break in my day, a chance to pour some love into my home, and they give me incidental exercise.

Hiring my lovely cleaner for the big jobs is an act of love. I'm giving her work and we get along well, chat and inspire each other. I know she contributes to my house with her grace. She's a yogi and a shaman and, in equal reciprocity, I know that she's getting the grace that's in my home.

The kids and I still do a certain amount ourselves because that is healthy. It's good for the children. It gives them important skills. Everyone should know how to clean up their own mess and look after themselves. We have a list of jobs to do and we tick them off daily. If you don't like being at home, live somewhere else or out of a suitcase. You can make wherever you are your home. Wherever you sleep, and wherever you spend your communal time, that is your home. You must respect it.

The home is a temple and to pull off transcendence, transformation and us being in the world you need somewhere to retreat. Everyone must have their retreat. I'm not asking you to walk off in the forest by yourself and discover God; I'm asking you to do it in your life, your suburban home. Right in the city, even if you're rural. Pull it off where you're at. You need daily cave time, though. You need to detox. You need, sometimes, a sabbatical. We need to bring back the Sabbath. Get plenty of sleep. Create the perfect sleeping environment. Make your home so gorgeous and fill it with so much grace that you won't want to go anywhere else.

## I simply do not have the time to spend on my home and rest and retreats.

Are you kidding me? Any time someone uses time as an excuse is a red flag. We are so screwed up by the concept of time. It has become our most precious commodity. I mean what is it about time?

I remember when I had my first crash and I went to an Ayurvedic doctor. He sat there, fumbling around and mumbling to himself. When he finally piped up he said, "You have an issue with time." He was dead right. Even though I knew what time was and that time was simply a dual experience, like all things manifest, I was still habitually stuck in the worldly approach to linear time. It was unconscious. This was a big breakthrough for me, learning and understanding what time is. I used to run late, get uptight rushing, squeeze more into my day and feel like time was my dominatrix. My partner was even worse. Not only did I have my own time issues, but his also. We were both spinning. Are you chasing your tail? Always late? Over scheduling your day? Have busy pride? Super Woman syndrome? This is not conducive to this way of being, of grace, elegance and peace. Get some help.

A She-Monk is spirit first and world second. You make the time. Work with the mindset that time is eternal. Something has to give. You need to cut a few branches off. Are you driving your kids around everywhere? Are you overworking? Do you need to cut back to three days a week at work? Whatever the case, you need to create time. Time is there and it is in your hands. A reshuffle is needed. Work on your wants and have faith that you will, in fact, be better off and thrive again once you stop abusing and chasing time.

We don't exclude the world as She-Monks. We use it as our teacher and our practice, but time out of the world is paramount. That's why I use the word 'monk'. We are monks. We just don't make all those crazy commitments, like poverty and chastity. I don't believe it's necessary to spend years tucked away. Unless it's natural and comes through you, then I think you're a legend. But don't force it on you and don't think it helps anyone in the world anymore at the level the world needs. Mind you, I did have an extraordinary opportunity to be a member of a spiritual community and centre. I can't recommend this experience highly enough to anyone on a spiritual journey. It taught me what I need to know to be able to do all this. Now I am dedicated to sharing it with you.

The world needs a huge injection of the sacred. The work we do creates a lot of energy. Our being, families and homes start to radiate. Imagine if our whole street was doing this kind of work. The street would radiate. Oh my god, it sounds like the beginning of world peace ...

The more collective energy, the greater the impact on our world. Imagine if we took this on? Let's look at your intentions, beliefs, goals, values, and schedule. Let's see where this concealment of grace is. Please don't try telling me you don't have time. There's something else going on and I won't accept it. It's time to stop and do an audit of your inner world and your belief systems. Time is eternal.

## A home retreat in my place is impossible. It's too busy and I don't like my home.

Okay, that's fine. Sometimes we live in a place that is far from perfect out of necessity, even though we put our best effort in. If there's no chance for you to organise a weekend for yourself, see if an obliging friend, a fellow She-Monk, can have you over to their house. There you can still be quiet, still be in separate rooms and do what you need to do. Maybe even do it together.

It may take time to get our lives set up for this, but if you have the love and dedication it will happen. It will fall into place. Don't stress; just get creative.

By the way, what don't you like about your home? Is there anything you can do to make it a temple? Can you make it beautiful? Can you move? Can you get help? Can you put something up? Light a candle? Maybe you can start burning incense? Anything to make it into a temple. If you manifest and pray for a new home or living arrangement, you will get what you want. Have faith.

You'll need that one day a week of lightness as a detox, as a minimum requirement to keep grounded and expanding in spiritual attainment. It's for healing, restoring and bringing about harmony and balance into our world, so it's important that your private space is beautiful and comfortable.

Make sure you also come to one of my annual retreats. That's where I nurture you and create one of the most wonderful spaces for peace and grace, and give all the practice and steps you need.

## Action Steps:

Plan and schedule. I make a plan every six months and have a weekend retreat every three months, if possible. If this is new to you then even once a year is a great start, but try to aim for at least two. Sometimes this won't come to pass – life does throw curveballs – but at least make this your intention. Create your retreat schedule yourself and start planning at least a month before. Start buying the things you need, cleaning the house and organising the other members of the home. They can go on a holiday for that weekend. Sometimes they can do it with you if they are of the right mind and inspiration.

Fill your home with the energy of your practice and devotion, with fragrance, light, music and mantra.

Know that the universe will support you to heal and rest, because that's what we're meant to do. We can't stop doing. If you're someone who has an achievement mindset and you don't want to sleep or eat – I wouldn't categorise you as a She-Monk right now. I think you're wonderful, though, and an amazing businessperson. I really hope you put that energy into a contribution for the world. That might be your purpose.

But otherwise, for those who don't have that iccha, that will, you're no less important and special. You'll be supported. Please learn to cook. Honestly, look at the gaps. What do you buy? When do you buy it? What do you feed your kids? What's your attitude when you cook? Most people I talk to can't stand cooking. That's so sad. Take it on as an art form. Take it on as mindfulness, as mindful as breathing. Take it on as transcendence, as the greatest act of love. You're nurturing your family. My children love home-cooked meals. If I'm really busy and have a week where we have to get take away for three or four nights they start to get really antsy. "Mum, can you please cook dinner!" I love that. Their systems are attuned to want healthy food, food with love. The love goes into their tummies and takes over their body. I'm not kidding. I'd be okay forever with simple daggy home food that's easy to assimilate and digest. Keep your master chef for the weekend or for your dinner parties. Simple changes often resolve a lot of our health issues and anxiety.

Once a year, commune with other She-Monks. Let's go on a retreat together! Join me. Let's get energised and inspired. I can teach you everything that I know. And please, never forget your daily practice. This daily consistency attracts consciousness. Schedule it in if you need to. I needed to because I had to take it on as self-love. Be consistent. Look at it like you would a job or career. For success we need committed time, every day, to be silent and be with grace. To do an audit of what has happened in our day or during the night, to go over and to let it go, so that we have a fresh approach each day when we wake up and so that we go to sleep without baggage.

We need this to transcend and transform.

> 'Our homes are a manifestation and representation of our energy. Make them a place of retreat, joy and harmony. Let them be beautiful, a place of expression, of who we are filled with grace.'
> **– Me**

# AFTERWORD

You're my hero.

You are the goddess, the universal mother, the She-Monk, the high priestess all rolled into one. That is my version of a superhero. I call my superhero 'Spanda Woman'. Someone who brings it all to the table and knows who they are. Someone who owns it and is happy to be humble, to be them. Someone who honours their calling to be devotional and of service to the world.

Most people read, get inspired then move onto the next thing. Spirituality is no different to any other aspect of our lives. The juice is in the implementation, the consistency and the dedication. The opening up to God stuff becomes the easy part, right? Why did we think it was so hard? But try bringing it back down to the world, back to being practical and talking about your experience. Can't find the words? That is because there really are no words.

We can only do the best we can.

We have to *be* the I AM. It's private, anyway. At a certain point we want to keep it to ourselves because it's so private and inexplicable to come face to face with God. Unless, of course, the desire to talk openly and candidly as best you can is called through you and out ;-) I like to cover all bases.

Every step is foundational and important. I took these exact steps. Once we get to the end we rinse and repeat. It is ongoing. Even my want has changed recently. I did another mandala and it expanded my world so much.

Start with where you are at. Recognise what is going on for you, who you are being, what the trigger is and what meaning have you given everything.

Be totally okay with it all. It's cosmic, believe it or not. Our human has just gone a little feral. Our mind had an off moment. That's being human. Don't worry.

Know why you're pulling away love or getting funky. You're not getting what you want. Or, as my mother used to say, you get everything you want but it's never quite as you expect.

Create a personal pledge. Write it out and look at it every day. Turn it into a passionate recitation every day while starting to keep the faith or meditate on it and take it in to work on the inside out.

Pay attention to what the universe wants of you and use your special gifts. Denying dharma leads to illness and depression. Please don't go there!

Forgive, meditate and open your heart. Look at judgments and do things for others. It's basic stuff, but it's where it's all at. Believe it or not, this is mystical. Mystical experiences happen as a result too. It works.

In my opinion, one of the most important parts is to really look at those spiritual myths we've inherited for generations, for centuries. Look at the stuff we've created ourselves and the beliefs we've trapped ourselves in while looking for approval and community. Ultimately, there is nothing but grace and how we experience it. Walk away from the crap.

Live creatively. Become responsible for the language you use, as it wires your brain. Start making better habits. The best way is through awareness and mantra. Go to the light and bring it back. Make your home beautiful. Make it a retreat, one worthy of being a temple for your magnificence self and those you love.

It's the best journey ever because it takes care of every aspect of our lives. We have made the world our teacher. What a brilliant setup!

We all need help at some stage. Watch for any spiritual ego that thinks we have to do it ourselves. Sure, we all have it in us, but it can get overwhelming and confusing without guidance.

Thank you for joining me on this journey. I look forward to helping you along the way, with whatever you need. Please feel free to email me with your questions.

There is no right or wrong way to go about this. These are the game-changers for me. They made my decades of intense and committed practice fall into place when moving back into the world. They were also the steps I took to heal physically, emotionally and karmically. I have certainly been through a mother load of karmas!

We never really finish. We simply move into the next phase of our evolution, whether we're enlightened or not. We may as well make the most of it. If you have the rare and tremendous fortune to get grace from a great being then blessed are you. That has the power to give you everything you need and only happens when you are open and ready. You do nothing. It is a gift. If you find a great teacher, be committed and do what they did, just like a business mentor. Then when it's time to move on do so. Never ever give up your power or give someone else control of your life.

I salute you.

Find the grace, do whatever it takes to hold it, be graceful, live gracefully.

# THANK YOU

To my family, my kids and friends. To the mentors, teachers and people of influence in my world that have supported me on my unique inner journey.

Most especially Barbara Stephens, Julia Renaud, Julie Deitz, Vanita Hayzelle.

To my book mentors Natasa and Stuart Denman.

To the crew at Busybird Publishing and Kev Howlett for the wonderful cover work.

To the grace of Bhagawan Nityananda who steers and mentors me today with tough love and gave my path to healing telling me 'to have the grace of an elephant'.

To my spiritual teacher, Swami Shankarananda, who gave me much of what I have today, from the many years of Satsang and listening to the works on Kashmir Shaivism that I adore and the stories of the great beings. Who inadvertently taught me through his own humanness what is of value and importance to me and how I wish to take what I have learned forward. I am forever grateful to have had such an excellent spiritual education that included a lot of love and a lot of heartache too. Sadhana is for the spiritual warriors.

To the sublime and wonderful teachings of Kashmir Shaivism that inspire me daily.

To my spiritual heroes that fill my well and who's teachings are my anchor: Anandamayi Ma, Ramana Maharshi, Bhagawan, Swami Ramdas, Narada, Swami Muktananda, Swami Lakshmanjoo, Nisargadatta Maharaj.

# ABOUT THE AUTHOR

Sally 'Lakshmi' Thurley discovered at an early age that there was a Self, an inner witness, someone part of something much greater than what was obvious. This led her on a lifetime pursuit of all things spirit and truthful. That God experience first came through the arts as an emotional connection. She then navigated an expat upbringing, a lifetime struggles of health, including disability, and the search for her own voice after surviving a domineering and dysfunctional childhood.

At sixteen one of her friend's mothers did a talk at Sally's boarding school. She spoke about Buddhist teachings and, in an example, suggested that we choose our own family. It was the first time Sally had heard a lesson about karma since her awakening as a young girl. It had a tremendous impact on her and fuelled her desire to know more.

After a long search, and after trying every faith and practice, from the church to new age, a twenty-five-year-old Sally finally came across an ashram run by a self-realised teacher in a wisdom yoga tradition. When Sally went for her first meditation class it was like coming home. Suddenly all her childhood experiences were there. Everything she knew deep down was explained and she dedicated her life to the study and practice for the next twenty years.

During this time, Sally had her two miracle children, became an expert in spiritual yogic cooking, became a hard-working single mum while doing her chef's apprenticeship and starting an entrepreneurial business called the Yoga of Food. She also became a Reiki master, studied to be a health coach and became an entrepreneur. She did years of training at the ashram and qualified in self-inquiry and meditation, becoming a facilitator of group and individual self-inquiry healing, meditation and coaching.

Sally has also been on pilgrimages to India where she contacted a great saint who has stayed with her in spirit, giving her the instruction, practices and commitment needed to lead her to spiritual answers.

In 2014 Sally's legs stopped moving overnight due to debilitating arthritis. Her world was turned upside down because of inexplicable illness. This was a deep and mystical experience, dressed up as a healing crisis. The universe took everything away from her one by one – her relationship, home, ashram and health. It became the culmination of everything she'd learned and took her to a whole new universal place. Fortunately she was helped by what she calls her 'spiritual angelic posse'. Sally was being healed from the inside out and learned what healing is all about. She came face to face with the darkest depression and discovered a light that is waiting when approached without fear.

Sally is a mystic and artist who honours her calling as an entrepreneur combining her experience, love and wisdom. She dedicates her life to bringing her gifts to the world so that they may help those who wish to find the grace in the world. She aspires to help others thrive soulfully and have the best life ever, and takes a special interest in those who are dedicated to self-realisation.

Sally holds offline and online meditation and healing groups, courses, workshops and retreats. She also does spiritual mentoring for those ready to find and live by their life purpose.

# MYSTICAL HEALING POWER SESSION
## SESSION PACKAGE

Have you wanted to break free from pain and suffering or being stuck but nothing has worked?

Do you want to know what the universal reason for your suffering?

Would you like to evoke the universal healing entities to work with you?

In your 1 hr Power session with me we will:

- Clear the space for universal healing and grace to enter
- Discover the divine assignment in the suffering or discomfort
- Find relief with a new perspective and soul connection.

*Value $150*
*Your Investment $49*
Email: info@sallythurley.com
With the subject line
'Mystical Healing Session'

# SOUL'S WANTS & HEART'S DESIRES
## SESSION PACKAGE

Would you like to know what it is you need to do to get what you want and stay on the path to enlightenment?

Are you ready to merge your world with what spirit is trying to work through you?

Want to find your unique spiritual practice and purpose in the world?

Email: info@sallythurley.com
With the subject line 'Soul's Want Session'

In your 1 hr session with me we will:

- Get clarity on what your heart and soul most want.
- Cut through the noise and stories in the mind to what consciousness is asking of you.
- Walk into the joy of living with the right aligned purpose and vision.

*Value $150*
*Your Investment $49*

# THE GOD EXPERIENCE

*Sally Lakshmi Thurley*

*Feeling it's time to know who you really are?*
*To know God, consciousness?*
*Been too busy and focused on life until now?*

- Learn the steps from suffering to Grace.
- The 7 Pillars of a foundational spiritual practice.
- Discover a meditation that suits you.
- Explore why you are here and where you are going.
- Learn the process of creation.

### Workshop Value $297

Special price $49 (3 spots per workshop for readers of this book)

**CODE: Book Workshop Special**

*Bonus: She-Monk book when you attend the event.*

**CONTACT:**
www.sallythurley.com
info@sallythurley.com
www.god-experience.com

# SPIRITUAL MENTORING PACKAGES

| WHAT'S INCLUDED | JOURNEY JUMP START (3M) | DIG DEEPER FLY HIGHER (6M) | ENLIGHTENED LIVING (12M) |
|---|---|---|---|
| Spiritual Mentoring Conversations One on One 45 Minutes Fortnightly | ✓ | ✓ | ✓ |
| Unlimited Email Support | ✓ | ✓ | ✓ |
| She Monk Book | ✓ | ✓ | ✓ |
| Compassion Workshop | ✓ | ✓ | ✓ |
| Meditation Masterclass | ✓ | ✓ | ✓ |
| Journal | ✓ | ✓ | ✓ |
| Mala Beads | ✓ | ✓ | ✓ |
| Meditation Shawl | | ✓ | ✓ |
| Book | | ✓ | ✓ |
| Life Purpose Workshop | | ✓ | ✓ |
| Meditation CD | | ✓ | ✓ |
| Calling on Divine Support Workshop | | ✓ | ✓ |
| Spiritual Healing Masterclass | | ✓ | ✓ |
| Meditation Asana Mat | | | ✓ |
| Spiritual Eating Audit | | | ✓ |
| Book | | | ✓ |
| Spiritual Food and Health Masterclass | | | ✓ |
| Anxiety to Grace Course | | | ✓ |
| The Power of Grace Retreat | | | ✓ |

After a life of intense spiritual search, overcoming personal traumatic obstacles, chronic illness, dedication to spiritual practice under a self-realized master and being called to take her spiritual experience and knowledge to the world, Sally is the ultimate spiritual mentor and teacher on how to live in the world embodying grace. Sally knows the level of dedication and commitment we need to be the I AM in the world and has not only all the mystical and yogic tools and practices, but has also successfully developed her own.

As a spiritual entrepreneur, Sally is passionate about working with people to find their experience of God, inner peace resulting in world peace and to finding the joy in their spiritual calling and taking it to the world as service to mankind. She knows from experience that suffering can be a divine calling, a spring board to hope, freedom and love and can be overcome.

## Sally Lakshmi Thurley

If you wish to invite Sally Lakshmi Thurley as a Guest Speaker at your event email us at info@sallythurley.com

**Sally is the Published Author of the book**

## She-Monk
### Our Daily Life is the New Spiritual Practice

Sally is available for speaking on the following topics:

**1. Mystical path to healing.**
- Finding the grace and universal message in suffering.
- The keys to healing our hearts.
- How to call on divine assistance, we are never alone.

**2. Spiritual transformation in the modern world.**
- How to use language to shift and transcend our story.
- Discover the transformation of holding God's vision.
- Live and love like the Dalai Lama while having a career, partner, kids and mortgage.

**3. Finding our souls calling as a doorway to purpose and joy.**
- Find your divine assignment.
- 3 ways to identify your calling.
- How to get the universe to give you everything you want.

www.sallythurley.com     info@sallythurley.com

www.ingramcontent.com/pod-product-compliance
Lightning Source LLC
Chambersburg PA
CBHW021103080526
44587CB00010B/360